Wonderland
English Literacy Programme

Get Set!

English Literacy Programme for Primary Schools

Stage Three – Book 1

✓CJFallon

Published by

CJ Fallon
Ground Floor – Block B
Liffey Valley Office Campus
Dublin 22

ISBN: 978-0-7144-1827-8

First Edition March 2012
This Reprint September 2016

Stories and poetry selected by Meriel McCord. Activities by Meriel McCord.

Fact units and activities by John Newman and Jim Halligan.
© Fact units John Newman and Jim Halligan

Design, Editorial Content and Activity Material
© CJ Fallon

Printed in Ireland by
Turner Print Group
Earl Street
Longford

Introduction

Get Set! is the first of two readers in **Stage Three** of the *Wonderland Literacy Programme*, which are designed for use in Middle Standards. Each reader contains 20 extracts from published children's literature, 10 fact units and 10 poems.

The published **extracts** have been carefully chosen by peer reviewers and cover a wide range of reading genres – classic, historic, contemporary, fact, humour, adventure, boy/girl, mystery/detective, and myth and legend. They have been graded to ensure an age-appropriate level of difficulty, with a gradual and continued progression. The works of a wide range of authors have been used so as to expose the pupils to as many different writing styles as possible. It is hoped that this will encourage the pupils to read the complete range of books, all of which are in print and readily available.

Each extract is followed by a series of **activities**, comprising oral language development, grammar/punctuation, comprehension, vocabulary, phonics and the writing process. There is a minimum of eight activities for each extract, with further activities included in the accompanying Teacher's Notes. All are designed in line with the Primary School Curriculum English Language Teachers' Guidelines (page 61): 'Children will need a consistent and structured experience of questioning, discussing, and probing the text in order to arrive at its full meaning.'

The 10 **fact units** and 10 **poems** alternate between the extracts and are thematically based, where appropriate. The fact units are followed by a comprehensive series of activities, which aim to test comprehension, develop vocabulary, stimulate creativity and encourage research skills. Fact boxes are used throughout to enrich the content. Activities on the 10 poems are included in the Teacher's Notes.

It is not intended that any children should write in their textbook. Rather, all activities should be done in their copybooks. Space-holding lines have been used in some activities to enable a wider range to be included in the reader than was otherwise possible (e.g. cloze procedures, etc).

The Teacher's Notes that accompany *Get Set!* feature a comprehensive week-by-week, month-by-month scheme outlining all elements included in the book. Oral language development, 20 extra poems, extension activities, drama and games based on the reading and factual material are also included.

Acknowledgements

The publishers gratefully acknowledge the following for permission to reproduce copyright material.

The Masked Pirate, reproduced from *Illustrated Stories for Children*, by permission of Usborne Publishing, 83–85 Saffron Hill, London EC1N 8RT, UK. www.usborne.com. Copyright © 2009 Usborne Publishing Ltd. *Tom Crean's Rabbit*, by Meredith Cooper, published by Frances Lincoln Ltd. Copyright © 2005. Reproduced by permission of Frances Lincoln Ltd. *The Diary of a Killer Cat*, by Anne Fine. Copyright © Anne Fine 1994, courtesy of Penguin Group (UK). Digital permission from David H Higham Literary, Film and TV Agents. *Fantastic Mr Fox*, by Roald Dahl. Published by Penguin Children's Books. Reprinted by kind permission of David H Higham Literary, Film and TV Agents. *Horrid Henry and the Bogey Babysitter*, by Francesca Simon. Text © Francesca Simon 2002. Illustrations © Tony Ross 2002. Reprinted by kind permission of Orion Children's Books, an imprint of the Orion Publishing Group, London. *Ignis*, by Gina Wilson. Published by Walker Books. © Gina Wilson. Reprinted by kind permission of David H Higham Literary, Film and TV Agents. *The Legend of the Worst Boy in the World* (Chapter 1), by Eoin Colfer. Puffin 2007. Copyright © Eoin Colfer 2007. *Her Mother's Face*, by Roddy Doyle. Text copyright © 2008 by Roddy Doyle. Reprinted by permission of Scholastic Inc. *The Christmas Miracle of Jonathan Toomey*. Text © 1995 Susan Wojciechowski. Illustrations © 1995 P.J. Lynch. From *The Christmas Miracle of Jonathan Toomey* by Susan Wojciechowski and Illustrated by P.J. Lynch. Reproduced by permission of Walker Books Ltd, London SE11 5HJ on behalf of Candlewick Press. *Sheltie and the Runaway*, by Peter Clover. © Peter Clover. Reprinted by kind permission of Penguin Books. Digital rights courtesy of Working Partners Ltd. *When Jessie Came Across the Sea*. Text © 1997 Amy Hest. Illustrations © 1997 P.J. Lynch. From *When Jessie Came Across the Sea* by Amy Hest and Illustrated by P.J. Lynch. Reproduced by permission of Walker Books Ltd, London SE11 5HJ on behalf of Candlewick Press. *War Game*, by Michael Foreman. Reproduced by kind permission of Anova Books. *Gulliver's Travels*, by Jonathan Swift. Copyright © Jonathan Swift. Ladybird Books Archive. Reproduced by kind permission of Penguin Books Ltd. *Oisín*. From *Irish Legends for Children*, by Yvonne Carroll, reproduced by permission of the publishers Gill & Macmillan. *The Carpet Bicycle*. From *Mr Majeika*, by Humphrey Carpenter. © Humphrey Carpenter. Reproduced by kind permission of Penguin Books Ltd. *A Blind Man Catches a Bird*. From *Folktales from Africa: The Girl who Married a Lion* by Alexander McCall Smith. Reproduced by kind permission of CanonGate Books Ltd. *The True Story of the Three Little Pigs and the Big Bad Wolf*, © Liam Farrell, 2001. Reprinted by kind permission of Mercier Press Ltd. Cork. *Wanted! The Hundred-Mile-An-Hour Dog*, by Jeremy Strong, published by Puffin Books. Reprinted by kind permission of David H Higham Literary, Film and TV Agents. *Spy Dog*, by Andrew Cope. Puffin 2005. Copyright © Andrew Cope 2005. Reproduced by kind permission of Penguin Books Ltd. *The Giant's Wife,* by Felicity Hayes McCoy. © Felicity Hayes McCoy. Reproduced by permission of Sheil Land Associates Ltd.

Poetry

I wish I was a Pirate, by Tony Bradman. Reproduced by permission of The Agency (London) Ltd. © 1991 Tony Bradman. First published by Oxford University Press. All rights reserved and enquiries to The Agency (London) Ltd, 24 Pottery Lane, London W11 4LZ. *The Dinosaur's Dinner* © 2005 June Crebbin. From *The Crocodile is Coming* by June Crebbin. Reproduced by permission of Walker Books Ltd, London SE11 5HJ. *Illustration not from original publication*. *The Ghost Teacher*, by Allan Ahlberg. From *Heard in the Playground* by Allan Ahlberg (Viking, 1989). Copyright © Allan Ahlberg, 1989. *The Guide Dog's Story*, © Wes Magee. reprinted by kind permission of the author Wes Magee. *Noises in the Night*, © Wes Magee. Reprinted by kind permission of the author Wes Magee. *The Sound Collector* from *Pillow Talk* by Roger McGough, reprinted by permission of Peters Fraser & Dunlop (www.petersfraserdunlop.com) on behalf of Roger McGough. *An Alien Shopping List*, by Ian Bland © Ian Bland. Reprinted by kind permission of the author.

Every effort has been made to secure permission to reproduce copyright material in this book. If the publishers have inadvertently overlooked any copyright holders, however, they will be pleased to come to a suitable arrangement with them at the earliest opportunity.

Contents

Get Set!

Stories, Poems and Fact Material

The Masked Pirate

Sam Sardine wants to be a sailor. He is very young but Captain Winkle trusts him to guard the ship's treasure. One night, Sam falls asleep and the treasure is stolen by the Masked Pirate. How will Sam find the treasure and capture the Masked Pirate?

Sam Sardine had always wanted to be a sailor.

He was desperate to travel the Seven Seas and do battle with bloodthirsty pirates.

As soon as he was old enough, he joined Captain Winkle's ship as a cabin boy.

But Sam soon found that life on board ship wasn't as exciting as he'd thought.

He spent all day ... mopping the decks ... peeling potatoes ... and washing the sailors' smelly socks.

Finally, he'd had enough. He went to the captain and asked for a proper sailor's job.

Captain Winkle thought Sam was rather rude. But he decided to put him to the test.

'All right,' he said. 'Let's see you sail the ship into port!'

Sam's chest swelled with pride as he took the wheel.

But steering a ship wasn't as easy as it looked.

Luckily, the ship wasn't too badly damaged. Sam begged for one more chance.

'Very well,' said Captain Winkle, at last. 'You can guard the ship's treasure.'

That night, while the rest of the sailors snored in their bunks, Sam sat guard.

But he was exhausted after his hard day's work. Soon, he was fast asleep as well.

Hours later, Sam was woken from his dreams by a wicked laugh.

He rushed up on deck, to see the dreaded Masked Pirate sailing off with Captain Winkle's treasure.

Sam felt terrible. What would the captain say? He didn't have to wait long to find out.

When Captain Winkle had calmed down, he offered a reward to whoever could track down the thief or his treasure.

But, as the pirate always wore a mask, no one knew what he looked like. Suddenly, Sam had an idea. 'I'll find the pirate *and* your treasure,' he said.

Captain Winkle didn't have much confidence in his cabin boy, but no one else had a plan.

That evening, Sam went to the Spyglass Inn, where the local pirates spent the night.

At breakfast next morning, Sam said in a loud voice, 'I heard the Masked Pirate talking in his sleep last night. He described the exact spot where he hides his treasure!'

One particular pirate sitting in a corner began to look worried. Sam's plan was working.

'Now I know where the treasure is, I'm going to get it for myself!' Sam went on.

Hearing this, the pirate rushed out of the inn. Sam followed close behind.

The pirate jumped into a
boat and rowed to an island
just off the coast.

Sam ran to Captain Winkle,
yelling, 'Follow that pirate!'

When they arrived on
the island, they found the
pirate hurriedly digging up
a treasure chest.

The captain recognised it at
once. It was *his* treasure chest.
Taking a flying leap, he landed
on the pirate.

'Take my ship and fetch help, Sam my boy!' he roared.
'You trust me to sail?' cried Sam. He grinned from ear
to ear. 'Aye aye, Captain!' he said.

The Masked Pirate, reproduced from *Illustrated Stories for Children*. Usborne Publishing Ltd.

I Wish I Was a Pirate

I wish I was a pirate,
With a long beard hanging down,
A cutlass dangling from my belt,
My teeth all black and brown.

A parrot on my shoulder,
A patch upon my eye,
A pirate ship to sail on,
A pirate flag to fly.

The rolling waves would be my home,
I'd live through many wrecks.
I'd always have the best of maps,
The ones marked with an X!

Pirates don't have parents,
They don't get sent to school.
They never have to take a bath,
For them there are no rules.

Yo-ho-ho me hearties!
It's a pirate life for me …
Pistols in my pockets,
Salt-pork for my tea!

Tony Bradman

Activities

Ⓐ Let's chat

1 What have you read about pirates?
2 What would you do if you were a pirate?

Ⓑ First impressions

My favourite part of the story is …

Ⓒ Seek and search

1 When did Sam join Captain Winkle's ship?
2 What did he ask the captain for?
3 Name the inn that Sam went to.
4 Who ran out of the inn?
5 Who leaped and landed on top of the Masked Pirate?

Ⓓ Quest and query

1 Why did Sam think that life on board the ship was not as exciting
   as he expected?
2 How do you think Captain Winkle felt when the treasure was stolen?
3 What was Sam's plan to catch the Masked Pirate?
4 Was Sam's plan to catch the Masked Pirate a good one?
5 Did Captain Winkle trust Sam after they captured the pirate?
   How do you know?

Ⓔ Word watch

A **synonym** is a word that is
close in meaning to another.

Match the words
that are synonyms.

ship	shore
deck	harbour
job	reward
port	large boat
coast	work
mask	floor on a ship
prize	disguise

8

F Sounds abound

Write the correct words ending in **st** or **ck**.

1 Pirates keep their treasure in this. ___ ___ ___st.

2 Shore. ___ ___ ___st.

3 To come at the end. ___ ___st.

4 You wear it on your foot. ___ ___ck.

5 Floor on a ship. ___ ___ck.

G Watch your Ps and Qs

A **sentence** is a group of words that must make sense.
It begins with a capital letter and ends with a full stop.

Which of the following are sentences? Write them in your copy.

1 The Masked Pirate sailed off with the Captain's treasure.

2 To put him to a test.

3 Sam's chest swelled with pride as he took the wheel.

4 The sailors snored in.

5 Sam's plan was working.

6 The pirate jumped into a boat.

H Flights of fancy

Imagine that you are a pirate. Complete the following sentences.

My name is _____. I am _____ years old.

My best friends are _____ and _____.

The name of my ship is _____. I hide my treasure _____.

I Spark starters

1 Find out about the 'Jolly Roger'.

2 Find out what you can about Blackbeard.

3 Find out what you can about Francis Drake.

Tom Crean's Rabbit

It is very cold in Antarctica, and the ship, *Terra Nova*, is crowded with animals and men. Tom the Sailor is looking for a quiet, cosy place for his pet rabbit to nest and have her babies.

HALLO, POLLY.

Tom the Sailor picked up Little Rabbit carefully in his big hands. He wrapped her in an old woolly jumper.

'You need a nest, Little Rabbit,' said Tom. 'Somewhere on this ship there is just the right place – warm and quiet and cosy. Let's go and find it.'

Tom the Sailor looked at the black cat with one white whisker. The ship's cat was tucked up in a warm, cosy place. He lay in his own little hammock, just like the sailors' hammocks, with his own little pillow and blanket.

'This hammock is full of black cat,' said Tom. 'There's no room for you here, Little Rabbit.'

Tom the Sailor looked up at the skylight where the ship's parrot was swinging on her perch.

'Hallo, Polly,' said Tom.

'Hallo, Polly,' said the parrot.

'You can't live on a perch, Little Rabbit,' said Tom, and gave the parrot a piece of string to unravel.

Carefully Tom the Sailor climbed down the ladder into the ship's hold. There were boxes and sacks and barrels, in stacks and heaps. It was very cold.

Tom peered around and shivered. 'It's much too cold and dark down here for you, Little Rabbit,' he said, and climbed back up again quickly.

Tom the Sailor looked into the big cabin. Everyone was busy hanging up paper lanterns, paper chains and flags.

'Come and help us put up the decorations!' they called. 'Come on, Tom.'

'Not now,' said Tom. 'I have to find a nest for my rabbit.'

Good smells were coming from the galley. Tom looked around the door. The cook was stirring something in a big saucepan.

'What's for dinner?' asked Tom.

'Special surprises for a special dinner,' said the cook. 'You just wait and see.'

Tom the Sailor put on his big, warm jacket. He pulled on his woolly hat and woolly gloves.

'We're going up on deck, Little Rabbit,' said Tom. 'Mind now, keep warm!'

Snow was falling gently. The sea was covered in big pieces of ice like white meringue. Icebergs floated slowly by, like spiky mountains.

Two whales lifted their great backs in a patch of blue-black water, then sank below the surface.

Fat, silvery seals lay on the ice, yawning and scratching themselves with their flippers. A little group of penguins stood staring at the ship. More penguins scurried across the ice in a long line. One penguin climbed to the top of an ice hill and the others pushed him off.

High above the deck, up against the sky, a wooden barrel was lashed to the mast. Pure white birds flew round and round the rigging.

'It's no good going up there with you, Little Rabbit,' said Tom. 'You can't climb, and you can't fly.'

The deck was filled with dogs. Brown dogs, hairy dogs, black and yellow dogs with pointy ears and curly tails.

Tom tucked Little Rabbit deep inside his jacket.

'Hallo, dogs!' said Tom. The dogs barked and yelped and howled.

Tom the Sailor went forward to the place where the ponies were kept in strong wooden stalls. The ponies were munching oats. They banged at the sides of their stalls with their sharp hooves.

'This ship is full up,' said Tom, 'it's crammed and crowded. Where can I find you a warm, quiet, cosy place for your nest, Little Rabbit?'

Little Rabbit's long, silky ears drooped.

'I've got it!' shouted Tom suddenly. He ran down eight steps, and poked his head into a gap under the deck where the hay for the ponies was stored. The air smelt sweet.

'Just the place for a nest!' said Tom. Carefully he unwrapped Little Rabbit from the old woolly jumper, and put her on to the hay. Little Rabbit hopped around, sniffed the hay, and lay down. 'And now,' said Tom happily, 'it's time for my Christmas dinner!'

Everyone sat down around the long table in the big cabin. They ate …

Tomato Soup
Roast Mutton
Plum Pudding
Mince Pies

Then they opened little parcels from their families. They pulled crackers, and played games, and sang songs. They were a very long way away from home, but it was a good Christmas party.

When it was nearly bedtime, Tom went to see if Little Rabbit was all right.

He poked his head into the gap under the deck where the hay was stored. Little Rabbit lay in her warm, cosy nest in the hay. Lying next to her were seventeen baby rabbits.

'That's the best Christmas present ever!' said Tom, happily. 'Seventeen babies! Now I can give a rabbit to each of my friends. Well, nearly!'

And he stroked Little Rabbit's long, silky ears.

Tom looked around at the night. The deck was covered in glittering snow. The world was utterly quiet and still. The sun was a soft golden ball, and the ice glowed white, with purple shadows.

'Happy Christmas,' said Tom to the world.

From *Tom Crean's Rabbit*, by Meredith Cooper.
Frances Lincoln Ltd.

Activities

A Let's chat

Have you ever been on a boat, aeroplane or ship? Where were you going? Who was with you? What happened?

B First impressions

I liked/disliked this story because …

C Seek and search

1 Who picked up Little Rabbit?
2 Where was the black cat?
3 What did Tom give to the parrot?
4 Name two animals Tom saw on the ice.
5 How many babies did the rabbit have?
6 Name three places Tom visited to search for a nest.

D Quest and query

1 Why did Tom not make the nest in the ship's hold?
2 Why do you think birds were flying around the rigging?
3 Why do you think there were dogs and ponies on board?
4 What time of year is it? How do you know?
5 How do you think Tom felt when he saw the baby rabbits?

E Word watch

Choose the word closest in meaning to the underlined word.
1 Tom <u>shivered</u> with the cold.
   (a) trembled, (b) moved, (c) shattered, (d) stood
2 The ponies were <u>munching</u> oats.
   (a) chopping, (b) tasting, (c) chewing, (d) drinking
3 The penguins <u>scurried</u> across the ice.
   (a) hurried, (b) jumped, (c) waddled, (d) hopped
4 Tom <u>peered</u> around the ship's hold.
   (a) walked, (b) moved, (c) looked, (d) climbed

Word

F Watch your Ps and Qs

Capital letters are used: at the beginning of a sentence; for the names of people (e.g. Ciara Ryan); for the names of cities (e.g. Cork), counties (e.g. Limerick) and countries (e.g. Ireland); and for the letter 'I' when talking about yourself.

Rewrite the following sentences using capital letters.

1 tom found a nest for little rabbit.
2 frank ryan and i went to the ship.
3 my dad saw lucy and jim on the way to school.
4 mary brady and adam daly are friends.
5 will i ask jack to come to the cinema?
6 dublin is the capital city of ireland.

G Sounds abound

Crack the code to find **sh** and **ch** words.

1	2	3	4	5	6	7	8	9	10	11	12
s	a	h	c	o	e	p	i	k	r	n	v

(a) 1,3,6 = _____

(b) 4,3,5,7 = _____

(c) 1,3,8,7 = _____

(d) 1,3,2,10,7 = _____

(e) 4,3,2,8,11 = _____

(f) 1,3,2,10,9 = _____

(g) 7,6,10,4,3 = _____

(h) 1,3,8,12,6,10 = _____

Write the code for

(i) cheese _____

(j) share _____

H Spark starters

1 Find Antarctica on a map.
2 Find out about Christopher Columbus and Marco Polo.
3 A ship floats on water. Find out if some items in your classroom float or sink, e.g. a pencil, a ball.

Rabbits

Rabbits in a field

FACT BOX

Pet rabbits usually live for up to nine years. However, rabbits living in the wild usually only live for about one year.

FACT BOX

Animals that sleep all day and hunt at night are called **nocturnal** animals.

Rabbits are gentle animals. They live together in families. Each family of rabbits lives in a hole called a **burrow**. Rabbits dig their **burrows** with their short front paws. Sometimes a lot of burrows join up together underground to make a **warren**.

Rabbits usually sleep in their burrows during the day. They come out mainly at night-time to feed in the fields. They love to eat grass. However, they like to eat most plants.

Foxes, stoats and hawks **prey** on rabbits. When rabbits leave their burrow, they must always be on the lookout for **predators**.

Rabbit in a burrow

When a rabbit sees a fox or another predator, it stamps one of its strong back legs on the ground. This warns the other rabbits that they are in danger. Then the rabbit runs back into its own burrow as fast as it can. A rabbit's tail is called a **scut**. It has a white tip. When the rabbit runs back into its burrow, its swishing white scut warns the other rabbits of danger.

Fox chasing its prey

Rabbit and its white tail (scut)

A litter of baby rabbits (kittens)

Male rabbits are called **bucks**. Female rabbits are called **does**. Young rabbits are called **kittens** (or **kits**). There are often six to eight kittens in a **litter**.

When kittens are born, they are deaf and blind and they have no fur. Two weeks later, they are running around. They can see, hear and have a soft coat of hair.

FACT BOX

There are many different breeds of pet rabbit. Some of the most popular are the **Dwarf Lop-Eared** rabbit and the **English Angora** rabbit.

Dwarf Lop-Eared rabbit

English Angora rabbit

drip bottle

litter tray

food tray

A rabbit hutch

Do you have a pet rabbit? Many people keep rabbits as pets. Pet rabbits are kept in **hutches**. This has space for the rabbit's food and **litter tray**. Pet rabbits are usually fed oats, mixed corn and bran. Sometimes they get a carrot as a treat. Too many carrots can upset their stomachs. The litter tray needs fresh sawdust or peat moss nearly every day. Most pet rabbits drink water from a **drip bottle**. Owners like these because the water does not spill.

Pet rabbits need exercise, so letting them run around in the garden is a good idea. They like to be petted and cuddled too. Maybe this is what makes them such popular pets.

FACT BOX

Not all rabbits are small. The **Flemish Giant** rabbit can weigh up to 7 kilograms!

Flemish Giant rabbit

Activities

24

A Talk about

1 Do you think it is right to keep rabbits as pets?
2 How should you look after pet rabbits?
3 Suggest some good names for pet rabbits.
4 Describe a young rabbit.

B What have you learned?

1 Where does a family of wild rabbits live?
2 What do you call a group of burrows that join up underground?
3 When do rabbits usually come out to feed?
4 What are (a) male and (b) female rabbits called?
5 Which animals prey on rabbits?
6 How do rabbits warn each other of danger?
7 Where is a good place to buy sawdust for the litter tray?
8 Why do you think rabbits prefer to hunt at night?
9 Do you think the white tip of a rabbit's tail is useful to them? Explain.
10 Why do you think that a rabbit grows fur?

C True or false

1 Female rabbits are called kittens. _____
2 Male rabbits are called bucks. _____
3 Young rabbits are called does. _____
4 Flemish Giants are a very large breed of rabbit. _____
5 Pet rabbits should only be fed carrots. _____

D What does it mean?

Finish the following sentences to show the meaning of the highlighted words.
1 A **nocturnal** animal is _____.
2 A **buck** rabbit is _____.
3 A rabbit's **scut** is _____.
4 A **predator** is _____.
5 A **warren** is _____.

E Complete the sentences

Rewrite this passage using the correct words from the box.

> day night nocturnal fox grass burrow stamps burrows
> danger doe kittens blind fur weeks hear

Rabbits are _____ animals. They sleep during the _____ in their _____ and come out to feed at _____. Rabbits eat mostly _____. When a rabbit sees a _____ or another predator, it _____ its back leg to warn other rabbits of the _____. Then it runs into its _____.

A _____ can have up to eight _____ in a litter. Rabbit kittens are born deaf and _____ and have no _____. After two _____ they are running around, able to see and _____.

F Look it up

Use an encyclopaedia/the Internet to answer the following questions.

1 In what way are hares and rabbits (a) alike and (b) different to each other?
2 Where do hares live?
3 Why do rabbits have such long ears?

G Finish the story

Here is the opening part of a story about a pet rabbit called Rosie.
Finish this story in your copy.

> **My Pet Rabbit**
>
> When I came home from school, I went straight outside to say hello to my pet rabbit, Rosie. What a shock I got to see the door of her hutch wide open and no sign of Rosie!

The Diary of a Killer Cat

Tuffy the cat finds the next-door neighbour's rabbit Thumper dead. He pushes the rabbit through the cat-flap of his own house. Tuffy's owner Ellie is horrified that the rabbit is dead. Ellie and her family think that Tuffy has killed the rabbit. They do not want the next-door neighbours to find out. Can they think of a plan to save Tuffy from being blamed?

Thursday

Okay, Okay! I'll try and explain about the rabbit. For starters, I don't think anyone's given me enough credit for getting it through the cat-flap. That was *not easy*. I can tell you, it took about an hour to get that rabbit through that little hole. That rabbit was downright *fat*. It was more like a pig than a rabbit, if you want my opinion.

Not that any of them cared what I thought. They were going mental.

'It's Thumper!' cried Ellie. 'It's next-door's Thumper!'

'Oh, Lordy!' said Ellie's father. 'Now we're in trouble. What are we going to do?'

Ellie's mother stared at me. 'How could a cat *do* that?' she asked. 'I mean, it's not like a tiny bird, or a mouse, or anything. That rabbit is the same size as Tuffy. They both weigh a *ton*.'

Nice. Very nice. This is my *family*, I'll have you know. Well, Ellie's family. But you take my point.

And Ellie, of course, freaked out. She went berserk.

'It's horrible,' she cried. '*Horrible*. I can't believe that Tuffy could have done that. Thumper's been next door for years and years and years.'

Sure. Thumper was a friend. I knew him well.

She turned on me.

'Tuffy! This is the end. That poor, poor rabbit. Look at him!'

And Thumper did look a bit of a mess, I admit it. I mean, most of it was only mud. And a few grass stains, I suppose. And there were quite a few bits of twig and stuff stuck in his fur. And he had a streak of oil on one ear. But no one gets dragged the whole way across a garden, and through a hedge, and over another garden, and through a freshly-oiled cat-flap, and ends up looking as if they're just off to a party.

And Thumper didn't care what he looked like. He was *dead*.

The rest of them minded, though. They minded a *lot*.

'What are we going to do?'

'Oh, this is dreadful. Next-door will never speak to us again.'

'We must think of something.'

And they did. I have to say, it was a brilliant plan, by any standards. First, Ellie's father fetched the bucket again, and filled it with warm soapy water. (He gave me a bit of a look as he did this, trying to make me feel guilty for the fact that he'd had to dip his hands in the old Fairy Liquid twice in one week. I just gave him my old 'I-am-not-impressed' stare back.)

Then Ellie's mother dunked Thumper in the bucket and gave him a nice bubbly wash and a swill-about. The water turned a pretty nasty brown colour. (All that mud.) And then, glaring at me as if it were all *my* fault, they tipped it down the sink and began over again with fresh soap suds.

Ellie was snivelling, of course.

'Do stop that, Ellie,' her mother said. 'It's getting on my nerves. If you want to do something useful, go and fetch the hairdrier.'

So Ellie trailed upstairs, still bawling her eyes out.

I sat on the top of the dresser, and watched them.

They up-ended poor Thumper and dunked him again in the bucket. (Good job he wasn't his old self. He'd have hated all this washing.) And when the water finally ran clear, they pulled him out and drained him.

Then they plonked him on newspaper, and gave Ellie the hairdrier.

'There you go,' they said. 'Fluff him up nicely.'

Well, she got right into it, I can tell you. That Ellie could grow up to be a real hot-shot hairdresser, the way she fluffed him up. I have to say, I never saw Thumper look so nice before, and he lived in next-door's hutch for years and years, and I saw him every day.

'Hiya, Thump,' I'd sort of nod at him as I strolled over the lawn to check out what was left in the feeding bowls further down the avenue.

'Hi, Tuff,' he'd sort of twitch back. Yes, we were good mates. We were pals. And so it was really nice to see him looking so spruced up and smart when Ellie had finished with him.

He looked *good*.

'What now?' said Ellie's father.

Ellie's mum gave him a look – the sort of look she sometimes gives me, only nicer.

'Oh, no,' he said. 'Not me. Oh, no, no, no, no, no.'

'It's you or me,' she said. 'And I can't go, can I?'

'Why not?' he said. 'You're smaller than I am. You can crawl through the hedge easier.'

That's when I realised what they had in mind. But what could I say? What could I do to stop them? To *explain*?

Nothing. I'm just a cat.

I sat and watched.

From *The Diary of a Killer Cat*, by Anne Fine. Penguin Group (UK).

30

Dad and the Cat and the Tree

This morning a cat got
Stuck in our tree.
Dad said, 'Right, just
Leave it to me.'

The tree was wobbly,
The tree was tall.
Mum said, 'For goodness
Sake don't fall!'

'Fall?' scoffed Dad,
'A climber like me?
Child's play, this is!
You wait and see.'

He got out the ladder
From the garden shed.
It slipped. He landed
In the flower bed.

'Never mind,' said Dad,
Brushing the dirt
Off his hair and his face
And his trousers and his shirt.

'We'll try Plan B. Stand
Out of the way!'
Mum said, 'Don't fall
Again, O.K.?'

'Fall again?' said Dad.
'Funny joke!'
Then he swung himself up
On a branch. It broke.

Dad landed wallop
Back on the deck.
Mum said, 'Stop it,
You'll break your neck!'

'Rubbish!' said Dad.
'Now we'll try Plan C.
Easy as winking
To a climber like me!'

Then he climbed up high
On the garden wall.
Guess what?
He *didn't fall*!

He gave a great leap and he
   landed flat
In the crook of the tree
   trunk right on the cat!
The cat gave a yell and
   sprang to the ground,
Pleased as punch to be safe
   and sound.
So it's smiling and smirking,
   smug as can be,
But poor old Dad's
Still stuck up the tree!

Kit Wright

31

Activities

(A) Let's chat

Have you ever been blamed for doing something you did not do? What happened? How did you feel?

(B) First impressions

As I read this story, I felt …

(C) Seek and search

1 On what day of the week did this story take place?
2 What did Tuffy push through the cat-flap?
3 Who freaked out? Why?
4 What did Ellie's father do?
5 With what did Ellie dry Thumper's fur?

(D) Quest and query

1 What do you think Tuffy meant when he said 'Good job he wasn't his old self. He'd have hated all this washing.'?
2 Tuffy's family thinks he has killed the rabbit. How do they try to make him feel guilty?
3 Who do you think will crawl through the hedge? Why?
4 What do you think is the next part of Ellie's parents' plan?

(E) Word watch

Who am I? Match the jobs with words from the box below.

> hairdresser   teacher   butcher   doctor   driver

1 I work in a hospital and treat sick people. _____

2 I teach in a school. _____

3 I drive a bus. _____

4 I sell meat. _____

5 I cut hair. _____

Word

F Watch your Ps and Qs

Singular means there is only one of something (e.g. dog).
Plural means there is more than one (e.g. days).

1 Write the plural form of each of these words.

Add 's'	Add 'es'	Change 'y' to 'i' and add 'es'
rabbit _____	box _____	pony _____
cat _____	glass _____	family _____
pirate _____	church _____	baby _____
sailor _____	fox _____	army _____
deck _____	hutch _____	berry _____

2 Write the following sentences in the plural form.

(a) The sailor looked at the pony.

(b) The rabbit munched carrots in the hutch.

(c) The family lifted the box.

G Sounds abound

When a word contains **tch**, the **t** is silent, e.g. stretch.

Write out every second letter in this word snake. Find five **tch** words.

H Flights of fancy

Draw a picture of what you think happened next in the story. Write two sentences about your picture.

Fantastic Mr Fox

Mr Fox has been stealing from the three farmers Boggis, Bunce and Bean. They are very angry with him. Carefully, they choose a place beside the hole that is the entrance to his den. The wind is blowing away from the hole. Will they shoot Mr Fox? Will he be hurt? Will he come home safe?

The Shooting

'Well, my darling,' said Mr Fox. 'What shall it be tonight?'

'I think we'll have duck tonight,' said Mrs Fox. 'Bring us two fat ducks, if you please. One for you and me, and one for the children.'

'Ducks it shall be!' said Mr Fox. 'Bunce's best!'

'Now do be careful,' said Mrs Fox.

'My darling,' said Mr Fox, 'I can smell those goons a mile away. I can even smell one from the other. Boggis gives off a filthy stink of rotten chicken-skins. Bunce reeks of goose-livers, and as for Bean, the fumes of apple cider hang around him like poisonous gases.'

'Yes, but just don't get careless,' said Mrs Fox. 'You know they'll be waiting for you, all three of them.'

'Don't you worry about me,' said Mr Fox. 'I'll see you later.'

But Mr Fox would not have been quite so cocky had he known exactly where the three farmers were waiting at that moment. They were just outside the entrance to the hole, each one crouching behind a tree with his gun loaded. And what is more, they had chosen their positions very carefully, making sure that the wind was not blowing from them towards the fox's hole. In fact, it was blowing in the opposite direction. There was no chance of them being 'smelled out'.

Mr Fox crept up the dark tunnel to the mouth of his hole. He poked his long handsome face out into the night air and sniffed once.

He moved an inch or two forward and stopped.

He sniffed again. He was always especially careful when coming out from his hole.

He inched forward a little more. The front half of his body was now in the open.

His black nose twitched from side to side, sniffing and sniffing for the scent of danger. He found none, and he was just about to go trotting forward into the wood when he heard or thought he heard a tiny noise, a soft rustling sound, as though someone had moved a foot ever so gently through a patch of dry leaves.

Mr Fox flattened his body against the ground and lay very still, his ears pricked. He waited a long time, but he heard nothing more.

'It must have been a field-mouse,' he told himself, 'or some other small animal.'

He crept a little further out of the hole … then further still. He was almost right out in the open now. He took a last careful look around. The wood was murky and very still. Somewhere in the sky the moon was shining.

Just then, his sharp night-eyes caught a glint of something bright behind a tree not far away. It was a small silver speck of moonlight shining on a polished surface. Mr Fox lay still, watching it. What on earth was it? Now it was moving. *It was coming up and up … Great heavens! It was the barrel of a gun!*

Quick as a whip, Mr Fox jumped back into his hole and at that same instant the entire wood seemed to explode around him. *Bang-bang! Bang-bang! Bang-bang!*

The smoke from the three guns floated upward in the night air. Boggis and Bunce and Bean came out from behind their trees and walked towards the hole.

'Did we get him?' said Bean.

One of them shone a flashlight on the hole, and there on the ground, in the circle of light, half in and half out of the hole, lay the poor tattered bloodstained remains of … a fox's tail. Bean picked it up.

'We got the tail but we missed the fox,' he said, tossing the thing away.

'Dang and blast!' said Boggis. 'We shot too late. We should have let fly the moment he poked his head out.'

'He won't be poking it out again in a hurry,' Bunce said.

Bean pulled a flask from his pocket and took a swig of cider. Then he said, 'It'll take three days at least before he gets hungry enough to come out again. I'm not sitting around here waiting for that. Let's dig him out.'

'Ah,' said Boggis. 'Now you're talking sense. We can dig him out in a couple of hours. We know he's there.'

'I reckon there's a whole family of them down that hole,' Bunce said.

'Then we'll have the lot,' said Bean. 'Get the shovels!'

From *Fantastic Mr Fox*, by Roald Dahl.
Penguin Children's Books.

Activities

A Let's chat

Mr Fox has to be very careful when he leaves his den.
We have to be very careful when we cross the road.
What must we do before and while crossing the road?

B First impressions

While reading the story, I felt sorry for …

C Seek and search

1 Name the three farmers.
2 What question did Mr Fox ask Mrs Fox?
3 Who farmed ducks?
4 Where were the three farmers waiting for Mr Fox?
5 How long did Boggis say it would take to dig out Mr Fox?

D Quest and query

1 Why do you think Mr Fox was always especially careful when
  coming out of the hole?
2 Which three sentences describe how the farmers smelled?
3 Did Mr Fox smell any scent of danger? Why not?
4 What senses does Mr Fox use in the story?
5 Was Mrs Fox worried about Mr Fox? How do you know?

E Word watch

Choose the odd one out in the following lists of words,
e.g. apple, pear, banana, <u>carrot</u>, peach.

1 ship, treasure, parrot, Jolly Roger, banana _____

2 hold, galley, bedroom, deck, mast _____

3 pony, cow, donkey, penguin, sheep _____

4 hutch, kennel, stable, ship, sty _____

5 clouds, sun, moon, trees, star _____

6 fox, goose, duck, turkey, chicken _____

Word

F Sounds abound

The 'ai' sound can be written as 'ai' or 'ay', e.g. sailor, day.

Write down as many words as you can using these letters.

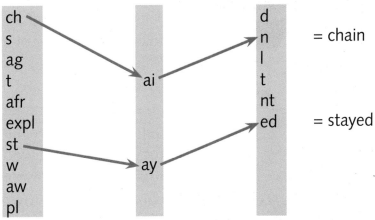

G Watch your Ps and Qs

Complete the following sentences by choosing the correct word from the box, e.g. Mr Fox was as **quick** as a whip.

| slow | busy | cold | wise | good | sweet | green | blind |

1 As _____ as a bat.

2 As _____ as a snail.

3 As _____ as ice.

4 As _____ as an owl.

5 As _____ as honey.

6 As _____ as a bee.

7 As _____ as grass.

8 As _____ as gold.

H Flights of fancy

A **paragraph** is a group of sentences written about one idea.

> There was no food for the foxes that night, and soon the children dozed off. Then Mrs Fox dozed. But Mr Fox couldn't sleep because of the pain in the stump of his tail. Suddenly he heard a noise.

Write a short paragraph that tells what might happen next. `Digital`

Wild Animals in Ireland

Ireland might not have the wild lions and zebras of Africa. However, there is still plenty of wildlife to be seen. Let's look at some of the wild animals living in the woods and fields of Ireland.

A fox

Foxes mainly come out at night. They are **nocturnal** animals. A male fox is called a **dog** or a **reynard**. A female fox is called a **vixen**. Young foxes are called **cubs**. Foxes live in an underground home called a **den** or **earth**. They hunt for their food in fields and woods. Some foxes have moved from the country to live in towns and cities. This, strangely, is because it is easier for them to find food in the rubbish bins that people have in their gardens.

Badgers are also nocturnal animals. Their black and white fur makes them difficult to see in the moonlight. Badgers live in an underground tunnel called a **sett**. A female badger is called a **sow**. A male is called a **boar**. A young badger is called a **cub**. Badgers are **omnivores**. This means they like to eat small animals, insects and plants. They find most of their food by digging up the ground with their strong front feet. They like digging in places with lots of trees. Like foxes, badgers have also begun to live in towns.

A badger

Stoats are long, slinky and fast hunters. They like to catch rabbits. They have sharp teeth and are very fierce. Their summer coat is a lovely red-brown colour. There is a black tip at the end of their long tails. Stoats like to live in the homes of the animals they kill. Sometimes they live in tree trunks, old outhouses, piles of logs or hay sheds. They even live in rubbish tips in back gardens.

A stoat

A pine marten

Pine martens are often confused with stoats. The main features of pine martens are their cream throat 'bibs', pointed muzzles and triangle-shaped ears. They have a brown-coloured face. Pine martens have a bushier tail than stoats. They live and hunt in woods, while stoats will hunt out in fields. Pine martens are very rare in Ireland.

Otters are also similar in shape to stoats. However, they are a lot bigger. They are great swimmers and spend a lot of time in rivers. They are very good at catching fish. They appear to enjoy playing in the water as much as hunting in it.

An otter

A red squirrel

A grey squirrel

There are two kinds of **squirrel** in Ireland: the red squirrel and its larger cousin, the grey squirrel. Some grey squirrels were brought here from America over 100 years ago as pets. They escaped and became wild. There are now more grey squirrels than red squirrels in Ireland. Squirrels like to eat nuts such as acorns and hazelnuts. They like to live in woods. Squirrels build their homes in trees. These are called **dreys**.

A hedgehog rolled into a ball to protect itself

A hedgehog

Hedgehogs hunt for insects, slugs and worms. They like to live where there are lots of trees. If a hedgehog is frightened, it will roll itself into a ball. This makes its sharp spines stick out, making it difficult for a predator to attack it.

A sika deer

A fallow deer

A red deer

Deer are the largest of Ireland's wild animals. There are three kinds of deer in Ireland: red deer, fallow deer and sika deer. They usually live in places where there are woods or forests.

FACT BOX

Some animals hibernate or sleep through the cold of winter. Hedgehogs will make a cosy nest of leaves and sleep until the spring.

Squirrels will sleep for a few weeks at a time. When they wake up, they collect the nuts that they have stored away to eat. Then they go back to their drey and sleep again.

There are about seven different types of bat in Ireland. They come out at night to hunt for insects. Bats hibernate through the winter.

Squirrel coming out of its drey

A hedgehog

A bat in a cave

Activities

Talk about

    1 Talk about wild animals in Ireland.

    2 Describe your favourite animal.

    3 Talk about any wild animal you have seen.

B **What have you learned?**

    1 What is a female fox called?

    2 What are animals that eat meat called?

    3 Name an animal that is an omnivore.

    4 Why have some foxes begun to live in towns and cities?

    5 Would you think that stoats are lazy? Explain.

    6 Why do you think otters are happier in water than on land?

    7 Name the smaller of the two types of squirrel that are found in Ireland.

    8 What is the largest wild animal in Ireland?

    9 Why do hedgehogs have sharp spines on their bodies?

  10 Which of the animals described would you like as a pet? Explain.

C **True or false**

    1 Foxes prefer the day time. _____

    2 Grey squirrels came to Ireland from America. _____

    3 A female fox is called a sow. _____

    4 Badgers live in a drey. _____

    5 There are three kinds of deer in Ireland. _____

    6 Rabbits store acorns and hazelnuts for the winter. _____

    7 Foxes look after their cubs in a den. _____

    8 Otters are great swimmers. _____

    9 Deer are the smallest of Ireland's wild animals. _____

  10 Hibernate means to sleep through the cold winter. _____

D Complete the sentences

Rewrite this passage using the correct words from the word box.

Ireland place down houses Badgers food
dreys leaves beat wake cold animals

In _____, the winter can be long and _____. Food can be hard to
find. Some Irish _____ hibernate. They find a nice, quiet and safe
_____. Then they go into a very, very deep sleep. Their hearts _____
very slowly. Hedgehogs hibernate in a nest of _____. Bats hang upside
_____ and hibernate in caves or old barns. They even hibernate in the
attics of old _____. _____ will sleep for a long time in their setts.
However, they have to _____ up after a while to find _____.
Squirrels also sleep for a few weeks at a time in their _____.

E Look it up

Use your library or the Internet to complete the following **similes**.

fox   mouse   dodo   ox   tortoise   lamb   wolf   owl

1 As strong as an _____.   **5** As slow as a _____.

2 As cute as a _____.   **6** As dead as a _____.

3 As wise as an _____.   **7** As gentle as a _____.

4 As quiet as a _____.   **8** As hungry as a _____.

F Finish the story

We were walking through the woods last Sunday. It was a lovely day
and we were having a great time. We were just turning back to go home
when I spotted a rabbit on the path just in front of us. Its paw was cut ...

Horrid Henry and the Bogey Babysitter

Horrid Henry's parents have gone out. He is left alone with a terrifying babysitter. Will Horrid Henry convince her to let him stay up late?

Rabid Rebecca switched off the light. 'Don't even think of moving from that bed,' she hissed. 'If I see you, or hear you, or even smell you, you'll be sorry you were born. I'll stay downstairs, you stay upstairs, and that way no one will get hurt.' Then she marched out of the room and slammed the door.

Horrid Henry was so shocked he could not move. He, Horrid Henry the bulldozer of babysitters, the terror of teachers, the bully of brothers, was in bed, lights out, at seven o'clock.

Seven o'clock! Two whole hours before his bedtime! This was an outrage! He could hear Moody Margaret shrieking next door. He could hear Toddler Tom zooming about on his tricycle. No one went to bed at seven o'clock. Not even toddlers!

Worst of all, he was thirsty. So what if she told me to stay in bed, thought Horrid Henry. I'm thirsty.

I'm going to go downstairs and get myself a glass of water. It's my house and I'll do what I want.

Horrid Henry did not move.

I'm dying of thirst here, thought Henry. Mum and Dad will come home and I'll be a dried out old stick insect, and boy will she be in trouble.

Horrid Henry still did not move.

Go on, feet, urged Henry, let's just step on down and get a little ol' glass of water. So what if that bogey babysitter said he had to stay in bed. What could she do to him?

She could chop off my head and bounce it down the stairs, thought Henry.

Eeek.

Well, let her try.

Horrid Henry remembered who he was. The boy who'd sent teachers shrieking from the classroom. The boy who'd destroyed the Demon Dinner Lady. The boy who had run away from home and almost reached the Congo.

I will get up and get a drink of water, he thought.

Sneak. Sneak. Sneak.

Horrid Henry crept to the bedroom door.

Slowly he opened it a crack.

Creak.

Then slowly, slowly, he opened the door a bit more and slipped out.

ARGHHHHHH!

There was Rabid Rebecca sitting at the top of the stairs.

It's a trap, thought Henry. She was lying in wait for me. I'm dead, I'm finished, they'll find my bones in the morning.

Horrid Henry dashed back inside his room and awaited his doom.

Silence.

What was going on? Why hadn't Rebecca torn him apart limb from limb?

Horrid Henry opened his door a fraction and peeped out.

Rabid Rebecca was still sitting huddled at the top of the stairs. She did not move. Her eyes were fixed straight ahead.

'Spi – spi – spider,' she whispered. She pointed at a big, hairy spider in front of her with a trembling hand.

'It's huge,' said Henry. 'Really hairy and horrible and wriggly and –'

'STOP!' squealed Rebecca. 'Help me, Henry,' she begged.

Horrid Henry was not the fearless leader of a pirate gang for nothing.

'If I risk my life and get rid of the spider, can I watch Mutant Max?' said Henry.

'Yes,' said Rebecca.

'And stay up 'til my parents come home?'

'Yes,' said Rebecca.

'And eat all the ice cream in the fridge?'

'YES!' shrieked Rebecca. 'Just get rid of that – that –'

'Deal,' said Horrid Henry.

He dashed to his room and grabbed a jar.

Rabid Rebecca hid her eyes as Horrid Henry scooped up the spider. What a beauty!

'It's gone,' said Henry.

Rebecca opened her beady red eyes.

'Right, back to bed, you little brat!'

'What?' said Henry.

'Bed. Now!' screeched Rebecca.

'But we agreed ...' said Henry.

'Tough,' said Rebecca. 'That was then.'

'Traitor,' said Henry.

He whipped out the spider jar from behind his back and unscrewed the lid.

'On guard!' he said.

'AAEEEE!' whimpered Rebecca.

Horrid Henry advanced menacingly towards her.

'NOOOOOOO!' wailed Rebecca, stepping back.

'Now get in that room and stay there,' ordered Henry. 'Or else.'

Rabid Rebecca skedaddled into the bathroom and locked the door.

'If I see you or hear you or even smell you you'll be sorry you were born,' said Henry.

'I already am,' said Rabid Rebecca.

Horrid Henry spent a lovely evening in front of the telly. He watched scary movies. He ate ice cream and sweets and biscuits and crisps until he could stuff no more in.

Vroom vroom.

Oops. Parents home.

Horrid Henry dashed upstairs and leapt into bed just as the front door opened.

Mum and Dad looked around the sitting room, littered with sweet wrappers, biscuit crumbs and ice cream cartons.

'You did tell her to help herself,' said Mum.

'Still,' said Dad. 'What a pig.'

'Never mind,' said Mum brightly, 'at least she managed to get Henry to bed.'

From *Horrid Henry and the Bogey Babysitter*, by Francesca Simon. Illustrations by Tony Ross. Orion Children's Books.

An Alien Shopping List

A solar-powered moon bike
An interstellar phone
An anti-matter sofa
For a crystal Martian home
A rocket-powered transporter
Irradiated shoes
Bioactive spectacles
Dehydrated stews
A supersonic spacesuit
An X-ray laser gun
Shopping for an alien
Is really lots of fun!

Ian Bland

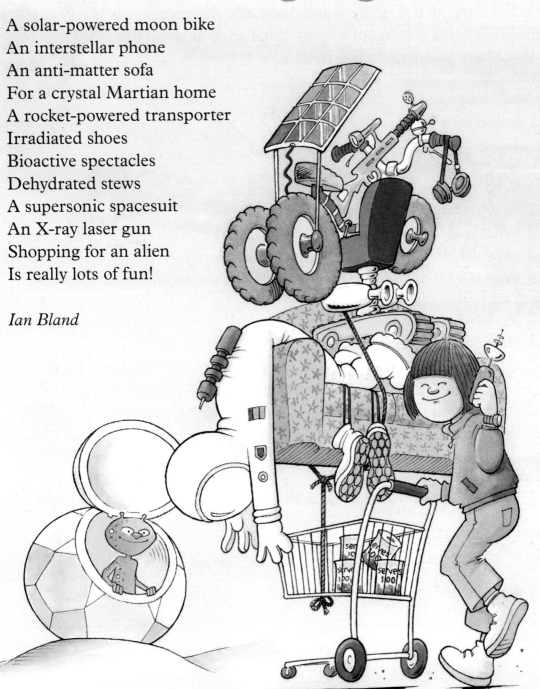

Activities

A Let's chat

In this story, Horrid Henry is afraid of Rabid Rebecca.
Rabid Rebecca is afraid of spiders. What are you afraid of?
What have you done to overcome your fear?

B First impressions

I wonder why …

C Seek and search

1 Who switched off the light?
2 At what time was Horrid Henry in bed?
3 What was Rabid Rebecca afraid of?
4 How did Horrid Henry spend the evening?
5 Who did Mum and Dad think had littered the room?

D Quest and query

1 How do you know Henry wasn't happy to be in bed?
2 Do you think he was really a fearless leader of a pirate gang? Explain.
3 If you were Rebecca, would you babysit Henry again? Why?
4 Who do you think is more clever: Rebecca or Henry? Why?
5 Why do you think Henry ran upstairs and leapt into bed?

E Word watch

Match the words from the box with the descriptions below.

hiss	spider	horrible	trembling
thirsty	urged	demon	outrage

1 eight-legged creature _____

2 shaking _____

3 nasty _____

4 sound a snake makes _____

5 in need of a drink _____

6 encouraged _____

7 anger _____

8 devil _____

F Watch your Ps and Qs

When a sentence asks a question, a question mark is placed at the
end, e.g. Who was babysitting Henry?

Write the following sentences properly.

1 rebecca was babysitting henry
2 who was frightened of spiders
3 henry spent the evening watching television
4 what room did his parents look around

G Sounds abound

The sitting room was littered with sweet wrappers and biscuit crumbs.
In this sentence, the **w** in wrappers and the **b** in crumbs are silent letters.

Are the following sentences true or false? Circle the silent letters.

1 A wren is a big bird. _____
2 Your thumb is a short, thick finger. _____
3 An arm or a leg is a limb. _____
4 A spider cannot climb. _____
5 Biscuit crumbs are big pieces of biscuit. _____

H Flights of fancy

1 Use words or sentences to describe Rabid Rebecca in boxes in your copy.

Name?	Is she big or small?	What is she wearing?
Describe her face.	Describe her hair.	What kind of person is she?

2 Use the words in the boxes to help you to write a paragraph describing
Rabid Rebecca. **Digital**

Ignis

Ignis, the young dragon, lives in Dragonland. He can run the fastest and fly the highest. But Ignis is sad. He has no fire. He thinks a dragon without fire is not a real dragon. He sets off on his journey trying to find his fire. As he meets his friends, he feels a warmth stirring deep inside him. Will he manage to find his fire?

Ignis lived with his sister, Flamma, and Gran-dragon. They had their own warm, dark cave in Dragonland, which is a secret place, no bigger than a village, hidden in rocks at the foot of a steep mountain.

Ignis had fiery red scales, flaring nostrils and a spiky tail. His wings, depending on the weather, opened like silk umbrellas or gossamer parasols.

His friends all admired him very much. Some even wished they were him, instead of themselves. He could run the fastest and fly the highest.

But Ignis was sad.

Every night, he sat at the back of the cave, huffing and puffing till he thought he would burst, but not a single flame ever appeared, not a flicker.

Gran-dragon stirred her pot. 'All in good time,' she said. 'Never worry.'

'Come and light stars with me,' said Flamma. 'You might just get the hang of it without thinking.'

But Ignis wasn't comforted. He couldn't light stars, and he couldn't start the cave fire to boil the kettle. He couldn't play *Fling a Flame* or *All Blaze Together*. He could only watch.

His best friend, Scintilla, watched with him. She warmed him with her amber eyes. 'I love you anyway.'

'I love you too,' said Ignis. 'But it's no good unless I find my fire. I don't feel like a dragon at all. Maybe I'm really something else.'

One dawn, Ignis set off into the thick forest that ran all the way round the foot of the mountain.

In the river he spotted Poto, floating along with just his eyes showing. 'Hello,' said Poto oozily. 'Come on in, if you like.'

So Ignis spent the morning slowly flowing with the current, and the afternoon caking his scales with mud. But by evening he knew he wasn't a hippo. His mouth was much too small and he was worried the water might rust his scales.

'You're a wonderful friend,' he told Poto, 'but I'll have to be on my way. I'm not really a hippo, you know.'

Poto laughed. 'I can see that, Little Puff-of-Smoke! You're a dragon!'

'But where's my fire?' said Ignis.

'Inside,' said Poto. 'Best place when you're swimming.'

Ignis waved goodbye. 'I won't forget you,' he called, and felt a friendly lick of flame flaring inside his chest. He gave a cough, and then another, but it wouldn't come out.

The next day, Ignis woke under a shady tree.

'Hello,' said Loquax from a branch. 'Come on up, if you like.'

So Ignis spent the morning flying between the sun and the treetops, and the afternoon shrieking his head off. But by evening he knew he wasn't a parrot. He hadn't got a beak and he wasn't tickling all over with feathers.

'You're a wonderful friend,' he told Loquax, 'but I'll have to be on my way. I'm not really a parrot, you know.'

Loquax laughed so heartily his best tail plume dropped out. 'I can see that, handsome Little Nostril-Nose! You're a dragon!'

'But where's my fire?' said Ignis.

'Inside,' said Loquax. 'Best place when you're flying.'
When Ignis waved Loquax goodbye, the heat in his chest felt like a sore, burning place. 'I'll never forget you,' he called, and sighed deeply, and sighed again. But still no flame came out.

Ignis travels on having many more adventures with his friends. He meets a girl called Cora and they form a very special friendship. Alone on the mountain-top under the stars, he discovers that he has fire deep within him. He has become a real dragon at last.

From *Ignis*, by Gina Wilson. Walker Books.

Activities

A Let's chat

Did you ever really want to do something but were unable to do it? Did you keep trying? Did you succeed? Explain.

B First impressions

I would like to know …

C Seek and search

1 Who did Ignis live with?
2 Why was Ignis sad?
3 What games could Ignis not play?
4 When did Ignis set off into the forest?
5 Name all the friends Ignis met.

D Quest and query

1 Was Ignis a popular dragon? How do you know?
2 Do dragons really light the stars at night? Explain.
3 How do we know that he has a flame inside?
4 Write down two differences between Ignis and Loquax.
5 Write down five words you would use to describe Ignis.

E Word watch

Write the following sentences correctly by removing the incorrect words, e.g. The man jumped over ~~under~~ the wall.

1 Ignis lived on with his sister and Gran-dragon.
2 His friends all hated admired him.
3 One dawn the Ignis set off into the thick forest.
4 He felt a flaring inside out his chest.
5 His chest flame felt like a sore, burning place.
6 By evening, he saw knew he was not a hippopotamus.
7 He told spent the afternoon shrieking his head off.

Word

F Sounds abound

Wh is used in many words that ask questions, e.g. **wh**en, **wh**ere, **wh**at, **wh**y, **wh**ich, **wh**o and **wh**ose.

A dragon visited your school. The school went on fire. You are a reporter. You ask a teacher some questions about what happened. She gave these answers. Write a question for each answer.

1 It had fiery red scales, flaring nostrils and a spiky tail.
2 It was called Flamma.
3 Flamma's flame set the school on fire.
4 I think it was an accident.
5 Flamma headed towards Longford.

G Flights of fancy

The **story setting** is the time and place in which it happens.

Describe Dragonland in circles in your copy. Use what you have written in the circles to write a paragraph about the story. **Digital**

Name the setting	I see	I hear

I smell	I feel	The weather

H Spark starters

1 Find out about the Chinese New Year and the dragon puppets that are used to celebrate it.
2 Find the words of the song *Puff the Magic Dragon*.

Dragons!

Stories about dragons have been told for thousands of years. Dragons appear in fairy tales and legends from all over the world, including Japan, England, China, Poland, India and Wales.

Years ago, the fossils of long-dead dinosaurs were found buried in China. People could see that these were the bones of very big animals. However, they did not know what they really were. Some people believe that this is where the legend of the dragon began. There are lots of stories about dragons in China. Pictures and statues of dragons are very popular there. When Chinese people want to celebrate, they sometimes dress up and dance in giant dragon costumes.

Chinese dragon dancers

Legend has it that a dragon would hatch like a chick from a giant egg. It would live for hundreds of years and grow very, very wise. It is said that dragons liked to live in deep, dark caves. They had wings and could fly long distances. They could also breathe out fire and could burn anyone or anything they did not like. In the legends, the last thing you wanted to meet was a cross dragon! Some dragons were supposed to be nice, but others were supposed to be really awful. The trouble was you never knew which was which until it started to breathe fire at you! Many dragons were greedy and liked to gather big piles of gold and treasure. They would lie on this treasure, using it as a bed.

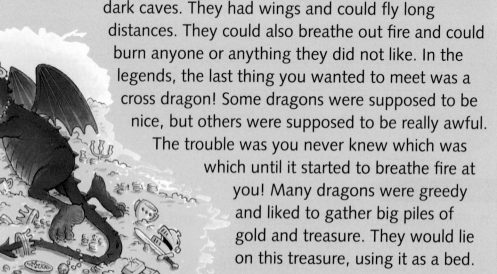

A sea dragon

There are many stories about dragons that liked to live in the sea. In the olden days, sailors used dragons as a way of explaining why some ships were lost at sea. Never mind storms, rocks, pirates or leaky ships. It was usually a nasty old dragon that sank the ship! For many years, sailors used to draw dragons on their maps and charts to remind them of the dangers of the sea. Sometimes, when they saw a whale in the distance, they mistook it for a dragon.

St George is the patron saint of England. Pictures usually show him with his sword in his hand, killing a dragon. The Welsh people are very fond of their red dragon, which flies proudly on their flag.

It is strange that stories about an animal that never existed have been around for so long. Dragons really only live in stories about adventures long ago. Maybe that is for the best!

The Welsh flag

St George and the dragon

Activities

A **Talk about**

The dragon in Ignis was a nice dragon. Can you think of a story in which the dragon was bad?

B **What have you learned?**

1 Name some countries that have stories about dragons.
2 What did Chinese people find buried long ago?
3 What do Chinese people sometimes do when they celebrate?
4 Where are dragons said to have lived?
5 Why do you think dragons lived in these dark places?
6 For what did the dragons use their fire?
7 What did the greedy dragons use as a bed?
8 Why did sailors draw dragons on their maps and charts?
9 Who is the patron saint of England?
10 How do you think you would feel if you met a dragon?

C **Mixed-up sentences**

Sort out the following mixed-up sentences.
1 for lived a long time. Dragons
2 liked They caves. to live in
3 treasure. gather gold and liked to Dragons
4 used dragons to maps. Sailors draw on their
5 patron is England. St George the saint of
6 their are fond people very dragon. Welsh of red
7 mistook dragon. Some a for a people whale
8 would an egg. A baby dragon from hatch

D **Sentence builder**

Using the phrases in the word box, write six sentences about dragons.

thick, scaly skin	razor-sharp fangs	gleaming golden eyes
scorching fire	huge claws	a puff of smoke

E Complete the sentences

Rewrite this passage using the correct words from the box.

egg	breathe	air	wings	cave	gold
ground	bed	wise	time	greedy	burn

A dragon was supposed to hatch from a giant _____. It had huge _____
and could fly through the _____ for a very long distance. Any dragon could
_____ fire and would _____ you to a crisp if it did not like you. It could
live for a very long _____. A dragon made its home in a _____ deep
under the _____. Some dragons loved _____ and would steal it wherever
they could. Then they would use the gold to make a _____ for themselves.
A dragon could be very, very _____. It could also be very, very _____.

F Look it up

Use the Internet or your library to help you answer the following questions.

1 Why is there a dragon on the Welsh flag?

2 When do Chinese people celebrate the New Year?

3 Chinese people call the New Year after 12 different animals in a cycle.
  Find the names of these animals.

4 Christopher Paolini and J.R.R. Tolkien both wrote books about dragons.
  Find some details about these books.

G Finish the story

We made our way through the long, dark tunnel of the cave.
We turned the corner. The tunnel opened up into a giant cavern.
We shone our flashlights and could see gold coins on the floor.
Then we saw the dragon lying on a pile of gold. It opened one eye,
looked at us and smiled …

The Legend of the Worst Boy in the World

Will has four brothers who all love to complain. Mum and Dad are so busy listening to his brothers' complaints that they do not have time to listen to Will. Will needs somebody who will listen to him. Can he find somebody who is a good listener and has lots of spare time?

It's not fair

I have four brothers, and they are always complaining about something. If I ever have a problem, and I go to my mum to talk about it, there are generally at least two brothers in the queue before me, moaning about something totally stupid. I could have an actual real problem like a hangnail or a missing sock, and there they

are wasting Mum's time with silly stuff like jam on their faces or back-to-front jumpers.

My four brothers have their favourite problems that they like to moan about at least once a day. Mum calls these problems their hobby horses. Whenever they start whinging on about them, Dad makes horsey noises and a here-we-go-again face, but Mum listens anyway because she's our mum.

Marty is the oldest brother, and his hobby horse is that he's never allowed do anything, and he might as well be in prison.

'Why can't I have a motorbike?' he often whines. 'I'm ten now and that's nearly sixteen. If I had a helmet on, the police would never notice.'

Or another one is: 'Why can't I have a full-sized snooker table in the garage? It's only full of old tools and a car, nothing important. I'll pay for the snooker table as soon as I become a famous football player.'

Dad sometimes comes into a room just to hear Marty complain about something. He says that Marty is far more entertaining than any television show.

'Snooker table,' Dad chuckles. 'Marty, my boy. You are cracking me up.'

This is not what Marty wants to hear, so he storms off sulking. Once when Marty came back after storming off, Dad presented him with a cardboard Oscar for best actor.

My name is Will and I'm the next in line. After me comes my second brother, Donnie, whose hobby horse is his hair. No matter how often Mum washes or combs it, there's always something wrong.

'It's sticking up at the back, Mum.' So Mum flattens the back.

'Now, Donnie, off you go.'

'It's still sticking up, Mum.'

'No, it isn't. You're having hair hallucinations, Donnie. Go on now, you'll be late for school.'

'I can see a hair sticking up. It's definitely there. The girls will see, and I'll get a nickname. Sticky-Up Woodman they'll call me. It'll be horrible.'

And so Mum gets out a water bottle and sprays Donnie's head.

'Better?'

'I suppose.'

This happens every second day. On the other days, Donnie wants his hair to stick up, because he thinks it's cool.

Brothers three and four, Bert and HP, have invented brand-new words so that they can whinge more efficiently. Bert's new word is 'canniva', as in: 'Canniva bar of chocolate?'

'Not before your dinner, honey,' says Mum.

'Canniva square, just one square.'

'No, honey. Dinner's on the way.'

'Canniva bag of crisps then?'

'I think you're missing the point, Bert. No sweets or crisps before your dinner.'

'Canniva throat sweet?'

'Throat sweets are still sweets, honey.'

Mum has great patience. Dad only puts up with two 'cannivas' before he gets annoyed.

HP (Half Pint) is the youngest and hates being the baby. The word he invented to complain about this is 'snoffair', as in: 'Snoffair. Chrissy's mummy allowed him to get his head shaved, now he looks at least five and a half.' He said this one afternoon after his half-day in baby infants.

'I'm not in charge of Chrissy,' said Mum. 'I'm only in charge of you. And I say, no head shaving.'

'Snoffair,' howled HP. 'Barry has a stick-on tattoo, like the big boys.'

'No stick-on tattoo. We've talked about this.'

'Snoffair,' muttered HP, then: 'What about an earring then? Loads of people have those. Snoffair that I don't have one.'

'Life's not fair sometimes,' said Mum, and hugs HP until he starts sucking his thumb. Two minutes later he is fast asleep.

Sometimes HP talks in his sleep. Guess what he says …

All this complaining means that by the time Marty and
I get home from school with our troubles there is usually
a little brother perched on each of Mum's knees, moaning
about their baby problems. And even if, miracle of
miracles, there is a free knee, Mum is usually on auto-nod
by then anyway. Auto-nod is when grown-ups don't really
listen to what a child says; they just nod every five seconds
or so until the child goes away.

So Marty and I decided that we had to target another grown-up to talk to about our problems. Dad was the next target, but sometimes he works so late that we don't even see him before bedtime. Marty reckoned that Dad only had time for one set of complaints, and that set should be his. So I had to pick someone else. Somebody who was a good listener and had a lot of spare time. I knew just the person.

Grandad.

From *The Legend of the Worst Boy in the World*, by Eoin Colfer. Puffin Books.

Distracted the Mother Said to Her Boy

Distracted the mother said to her boy,
'Do you try to upset and perplex and annoy?
Now, give me four reasons – and don't play the fool –
Why you shouldn't get up and get ready for school.'

Her son replied slowly, 'Well, mother, you see,
I can't stand the teachers and they detest me;
And there isn't a boy or a girl in the place
That I like or, in turn, that delights in my face.'

'And I'll give you two reasons,' she said, 'why you ought
Get yourself off to school before you get caught;
Because, first, you are forty, and, next, you young fool,
It's your job to be there.
You're the head of the school.'

Gregory Harrison

Activities

A Let's chat

How many children are in your family? What do you think are the advantages/disadvantages of having a big family?

B First impressions

The funniest part of this story is …

C Seek and search

1 How many brothers does Will have?
2 What does Mum call their problems?
3 Name the oldest brother.
4 Who is the youngest member of the family?
5 When does Mum go on auto-nod?
6 Where is Dad usually when the boys want to talk to him?

D Quest and query

1 How would you feel if you were Will? Why?
2 Name two words invented by Bert and HP.
3 What is meant by the phrase 'You are cracking me up'?
4 What do you think Will wants to talk to Grandad about?
5 Which character in this story would you like to be? Why?
6 Invent your own new word and explain what it means.

E Word watch

Choose the most suitable word to complete each sentence.

1 Dad thinks Marty is more _____ than any television show.
   (a) boring, (b) annoying, (c) amusing, (d) famous

2 Bert and HP have _____ new words.
   (a) invented, (b) spoken, (c) read, (d) learned

3 Dad only had time for one set of _____.
   (a) rules, (b) complaints, (c) ideas, (d) jokes

Word

F Watch your Ps and Qs

A **noun** is the name of a person (e.g. Mark), place
(e.g. Longford), animal (e.g. dog) or thing (e.g. table).

Write each of the following nouns under the correct
heading: **person**, **place**, **animal** or **thing**.

Marty	chair	Dublin	rabbit	piano	
Katie	France	cat	Ireland	Jack	Sarah
Cork	elephant	computer	snake	book	

G Sounds abound

1 Th can be **voiced** (e.g. them) or **unvoiced** (e.g. thumb).

Say the following words out loud. Write them under the correct headings:
voiced or **unvoiced**.

| they | their | Thumper | thin | there | this | thumb |
| thief | think | then | that | thought | these | with |

2 Tricky words: **there** or **their**

Complete the following sentences with 'There/there' or 'Their/their'.

(a) Will's brothers have _____ favourite problems.

(b) _____ are five boys in _____ family.

(c) _____ is _____ Grandad over _____.

(d) _____ mother told them to eat over _____.

(e) 'Stand over _____,' said _____ mother.

(f) '_____ are 12 eggs in a dozen,' said _____ teacher.

H Flights of fancy

Choose one brother from the story. In your own words,
write down what he was complaining about.

Her Mother's Face

Siobhán and her father live in Dublin. They are both sad because Siobhán's mother has died. They do not talk about her. Siobhán is scared that the memories of her mother are fading. She meets a beautiful woman in a park who gives her some advice that will help her remember her mother.

There was once this girl and her name was Siobhán. She lived in a big house in Dublin with her father. It was a great house, full of interesting rooms and corners, full of old magazines and old machines and old, old toys and teddy bears. Siobhán spent hours and hours exploring the rooms and halls, and she always found something new. She loved the house.

Her mother had died when Siobhán was only three. She had no sisters and no brothers, no uncles, aunts, or cousins, and no grandparents. There was just Siobhán and her father. He was a nice man, but he was very quiet and sad, and he kept himself to himself.

He read to Siobhán sometimes. He brought her home a new book every Friday. He smiled whenever he saw her looking at him, but he never spoke to her about her mother. In fact, nobody ever spoke to Siobhán about her mother.

Siobhán was ten now, and she could not remember her mother's face. She had searched every corner of the house. She found her mother's old books and a scarf and a pair of mad green shoes, but she never found a photograph.

Siobhán could remember her mother's hands. Her hands combing Siobhán's hair, her hands peeling an apple, holding the steering wheel, pulling up Siobhán's sock, and her hands on her lap when Siobhán was brought into the dark room to say goodbye to her.

When Siobhán closed her eyes, she could see her mother's hands doing these things and other things but, no matter how hard she tried or how long she kept her eyes closed, she couldn't see her mother's face.

She could remember her mother's voice. And she could remember some words.

'Cat and spuds for dinner, Siobhán. How does that sound?'

'Yeuk.'

'Yeuk, cat? Or yeuk, spuds?'

'Yeuk, cat.'

'Okay. We'll have chicken instead.'

And she could remember her mother singing, 'Did you ever shove your granny off the bus?' She could hear her mother, but she could never see her face.

The empty space where her mother's face should have been was like a pain, a giant unhappiness that Siobhán carried with her everywhere.

When she saw other mothers hugging their children, or buttoning their coats, and even when she saw her friends' mothers yelling at her friends, the pain grew in her chest and pushed up tears to her eyes. And, as she got older, the pain got worse and worse, because her mother seemed to be going further and further away.

Other children liked Siobhán. They liked sitting beside her in school. She never argued, and she never whinged or grabbed and broke things. She made them laugh. She would cross her eyes and say the things that adults love saying.

'Money doesn't grow on trees.'

'It's raining cats and dogs.'

'I have eyes in the back of my head.'

Her friends all knew that Siobhán's mother was dead, but none of them knew how sad she was. She never told them, and she never let them see.

When she tried to talk to her father about her mother, his face would fill with worry and sadness, and she'd stop. He hugged her once and said, 'Sorry.' They had a pizza and watched telly together. It was nice, but they didn't talk.

One day, Siobhán was sitting in Saint Anne's Park, very near her house. She sat under a huge chestnut tree. She could remember her mother's hands holding her up, high enough to pull a conker from the lowest branch. She could remember the voice.

'The big one, the big one. Grab it. Yesss!'

She could remember how it felt, the hands squeezing through her coat and dress, the nice safe feeling, knowing that she wouldn't fall. She tried to remember turning to smile at her mother, but she couldn't. This was what Siobhán was doing, trying to remember, when she heard a voice.

'Hello.'

Siobhán looked and saw a beautiful woman standing beside her. The woman sat straight down on the grass. Most adults never did this, because it was quite mucky and damp.

'You're sad, aren't you?' said the beautiful woman.

She had dark brown hair, like Siobhán's, and brown eyes. And she had a friendly smile and a lovely voice. Siobhán never spoke to strangers, but this woman didn't seem like a stranger.

'Yes,' said Siobhán. 'I am sad. A bit.'

'Why?' said the woman.

And Siobhán told her. She told her everything. About her mother's death, and her hands, and about how she could never see her mother's face. And she cried as she spoke, but she didn't mind. She just kept talking.

The woman listened, and smiled.

'You know what you should do?' she said when Siobhán had finished talking.

'What?' said Siobhán.

The woman wiped Siobhán's eyes with the sleeve of her jumper.

'You should look in the mirror,' said the woman.

'Why?' said Siobhán.

'Because then you'll see your mother,' said the woman. 'You'll see the way she looked when she was your age. And, as you get older, you'll see what your mother looked like when she was getting older.'

Then she kissed Siobhán, and hugged her.

From *Her Mother's Face*, by Roddy Doyle. Scholastic Inc.

Activities

A Let's chat

Have you ever lost someone special? Is there someone you can talk to about them? Can you remember a happy time that you shared together?

B First impressions

My favourite moment in the story was …

C Seek and search

1 Where did Siobhán live?
2 What happened to Siobhán's mother?
3 What could Siobhán not remember about her mother?
4 When did the pain in her chest get worse?
5 What advice did the woman in the park give to her?

D Quest and query

1 Why do you think Siobhán's father did not talk about her mother?
2 How did he show Siobhán that he cared about her?
3 Who do you think the woman in the park was? Why?
4 Why do you think Siobhán never let her friends see her sad?
5 What do you think Siobhán will remember when she looks in the mirror?

E Word watch

The following phrases are called **idioms**.

Write down what each of the following idioms means.

1 Money doesn't grow on trees.
2 It's raining cats and dogs.
3 I have eyes in the back of my head.
4 It would make your hair stand on end.

HER MOTHER'S FACE

F Watch your Ps and Qs

A and An

Usually, we use the word **an** before words beginning with a vowel (a, e, i, o, u), e.g. an egg. We use the word **a** before words beginning with a consonant (e.g. b, c, d …), e.g. a photograph.

Write the following sentences correctly.

1 The house had a interesting room with a old fireplace.
2 In her hands she held a apple and an sandwich.
3 She pulled an conker from an chestnut tree.
4 A iceberg and an penguin floated in the sea.
5 A alien had an shopping list in his pocket.

G Sounds abound

Match each **ph** word on the left with its meaning on the right.

1 dolphin	(a) a ball shape
2 photograph	(b) large silver-grey sea mammal
3 telephone	(c) large grey land animal
4 elephant	(d) a picture taken with a camera
5 sphere	(e) you can talk to people on this

H Flights of fancy

Do you think Siobhán felt happier after talking to the woman in the park? What will she tell her father? Write your own ending for this story. Digital

I Spark starters

Collect some photographs or pictures of people. Write about the photographs. Who are the people? How are they feeling? Think about their families, jobs, friends and hobbies.

Water

The Blue Planet

Photographs of Earth taken from outer space show a beautiful blue planet. Earth looks blue because it is mostly covered by water. More than two-thirds of the planet is covered with water.

The Earth as seen from space

The Oceans and the Seas

Most of the water on earth is found in the oceans and the seas. The water in the oceans and the seas is salty. Because of this, it is undrinkable. The **Pacific Ocean** is the largest of the five oceans. If you look at the Pacific Ocean on a globe or map, you will see that it covers almost half of the world. The **Atlantic Ocean**, which touches the west coast of Ireland, is the second largest ocean. On the other side of the Atlantic Ocean are North, Central and South America. The other great oceans of the world are the **Indian Ocean**, the **Arctic Ocean** and the **Southern Ocean.**

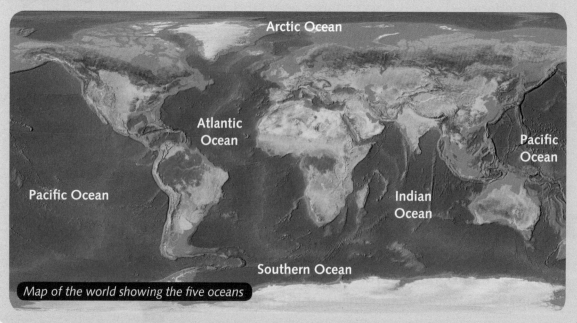

Arctic Ocean

Atlantic Ocean

Pacific Ocean

Pacific Ocean

Indian Ocean

Southern Ocean

Map of the world showing the five oceans

There are also many seas around the world. The **Irish Sea** lies between Ireland and Britain. The **Dead Sea**, in the Middle East, is so salty that it is very hard to swim in it! It is nearly impossible to sink in and very easy to float in. It is called the Dead Sea because fish and plant life cannot live in it.

Woman reading a book while floating in the Dead Sea

Rivers, Lakes and Streams

The water in rivers, lakes and streams is usually not salty. We call this **fresh** water. If it is clean, we can drink it. The water that comes out of taps is usually from a **reservoir**. These are special lakes that are used to store drinking water. Rain keeps the lakes and rivers full of fresh water. This may seem a little odd because most of the rainwater comes from the oceans and the seas, which are salty!

Not all lakes have fresh water. The Great Salt Lake in the state of Utah in the USA is a salt water lake. It is sometimes referred to as the Dead Sea of America.

A freshwater reservoir

Water

The Water Cycle

When the sun shines on an ocean or sea, it turns the water into water vapour (or steam). This vapour rises. The salt in the water is too heavy to rise, so it is left behind. The water vapour forms clouds. The wind blows the clouds in over the land. As the clouds rise, they

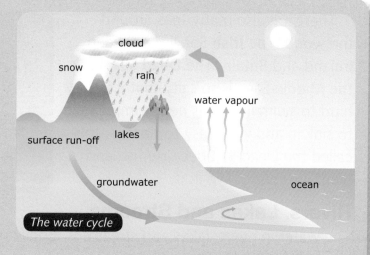
The water cycle

get cold and turn back into water. This water falls from the sky to the Earth in the form of rain. Some of it flows into the rivers and the lakes and the water cycle starts again.

Ice, Water and Steam

When water freezes, it turns to ice. The huge **glaciers** around the North Pole are, in fact, giant ice cubes. When water is boiled, it turns to steam. The first trains were powered by steam from boiling water. They were called steam engines. The most famous steam engine was Stephenson's 'Rocket'. It was built in 1829. It is strange that they called it 'The Rocket' as it only travelled at about 20 kilometres per hour.

A steam train

A glacier

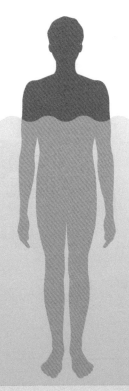
Humans are made of about 66 per cent water

The Importance of Water

Without water, we could not survive. In fact, much of the human body is made up of water. Like humans, all plants and animals need water to survive. Plants soak up water from the ground through their roots. Fruit and vegetables are also mostly made of water. We not only drink water – we cook with it, we swim in it, we clean ourselves with it, we sail in it, we eat the fish that live in it, we play in it, and we even make electricity out of it. Water is wonderful!

Image showing what happens to an apple as it dries out

Children having fun in water

Activities

A **Talk about**

1 Why must we drink water every day? How much water should we drink?
2 Why is it important that drinking water is kept clean?

B **What have you learned?**

1 Why is the Earth called the 'Blue Planet'?
2 Which is the largest ocean in the world?
3 Which ocean lies off the west coast of Ireland?
4 Why is sea water undrinkable?
5 How did the Dead Sea get its name?
6 What happens when water freezes?
7 What happens when water is boiled?
8 How do plants get their water?
9 Why is it a good idea to store water in a reservoir?
10 What do you think is the most valuable use of water?

C **True or false**

1 The Indian Ocean is the largest ocean in the world. _____
2 Raindrops are salty. _____
3 We should not drink water from an ocean. _____
4 The water in most houses comes from a reservoir. _____
5 Steam engines ran on petrol. _____

D **Sequencing**

Put the following sentences in the correct order.
1 The clouds get cold and turn back into water.
2 The water vapour forms clouds.
3 The sun shines on the sea and turns the water into water vapour.
4 This water falls out of the sky as rain.
5 The wind blows the clouds in over the land.

E **A water experiment**

How to separate salt from water:

1 Mix some salt into a cup of warm water.

2 Pour the salty water onto a saucer.

3 Leave the saucer on a sunny window sill for a few days.

4 See what is left when all the water has evaporated.

F **Complete the sentences**

Rewrite this passage using the correct words from the box.

| Pacific | steam engines | Indian | Arctic | Irish | ice |
| steam | Southern | Atlantic | water | blue | Britain |

Earth looks _____ from space because it has so much _____.

The largest ocean is the _____ Ocean. The other four oceans are

the _____, the _____, the _____ and the _____.

The _____ Sea separates Ireland and _____.

When water freezes, it turns to _____. When water boils, it turns

to _____. The first trains were called _____ _____

because they ran on boiling water.

G **Look it up**

Use an encyclopaedia or the Internet to answer the following questions.

1 Where was Stephenson's 'Rocket' built? Why was it so important?

2 What happens to fruit (like apples) when it is dried out?

3 What does a water diviner do?

4 Do camels store water in their hump(s)?

The Christmas Miracle of Jonathan Toomey

Jonathan Toomey was once a happy man with a wife and a baby. However, since their deaths, he has turned cold and hard. The children call him Mr Gloomy. One day, the widow McDowell and her son Thomas ask him to make a set of nativity figures. The miracle begins.

The village children called him Mr Gloomy. But, in fact, his name was Toomey, Mr Jonathan Toomey. And though it's not kind to call people names, this one fitted quite well. For Jonathan Toomey seldom smiled and never laughed. He went about mumbling and grumbling, muttering and sputtering, grumping and griping. He complained that the church bells rang too often, that the birds sang too shrilly, that the children played too loudly.

Mr Toomey was a wood-carver. Some said he was the best wood-carver in the whole valley. He spent his days sitting at a workbench, carving beautiful shapes from blocks of pine and hickory and chestnut wood. After supper, he sat in a straight-backed chair near the fireplace, smoking his pipe and staring into the flames.

Jonathan Toomey wasn't an old man, but if you saw him, you might think he was, the way he walked bent forwards with his head down. You wouldn't notice his eyes, the clear blue of an August sky. And you wouldn't see the dimple on his chin, since his face was mostly hidden under a shaggy, untrimmed beard, speckled with

sawdust and wood shavings and, depending on what he'd eaten that day, crumbs of bread or a bit of potato or dried gravy.

The village people didn't know it, but there was a reason for his gloom, a reason for his grumbling, a reason why he walked hunched over, as if carrying a great weight on his shoulders. Some years earlier, when Jonathan Toomey was young and full of life and full of love, his wife and baby had become very ill. And, because those were the days before hospitals and medicines and skilled doctors, his wife and baby had died, three days apart from each other.

So Jonathan Toomey had packed his belongings into a wagon and travelled till his tears stopped. He settled into a tiny house at the edge of a village to do his wood-carving.

One day in early December, there was a knock at Jonathan's door. Mumbling and grumbling, he went to answer it. There stood a woman and a young boy.

'I'm the widow McDowell. I'm new to your village. This is my son, Thomas,' the woman said.

'I'm seven and I know how to whistle,' said Thomas.

'Whistling is pish-posh,' said the wood-carver gruffly.

'I need something carved,' said the woman and she told Jonathan about a very special set of Christmas figures her grandfather had carved for her when she was a girl.

'After I moved here, I discovered that they were lost,' she explained. 'I had hoped that by some miracle I would find them again, but it hasn't happened.'

'There are no such things as miracles,' the wood-carver told her. 'Now, could you describe the figures for me?'

'There were sheep,' she told him.

'Two of them, with curly wool,' added Thomas.

'Yes, two,' said the widow, 'and a cow, an angel, Mary, Joseph, the Baby Jesus, and the Wise Men.'

'Three of them,' added Thomas.

'Will you take the job?' asked the widow McDowell.

'I will.'

'I'm grateful. How soon can you have them ready?'

'They will be ready when they are ready,' he said.

'But I must have them by Christmas. They mean very much to me. I can't remember a Christmas without them.'

'Christmas is pish-posh,' said Jonathan gruffly and he shut the door.

The following week there was a knock at the wood-carver's door. Muttering and sputtering, he went to answer it. There stood the widow McDowell and Thomas.

'Excuse me,' said the widow, 'but Thomas has been begging to come and watch you work. He says he wants to be a wood-carver when he grows up and would like to watch you since you are the best in the valley.'

'I'll be quiet. You won't even know I'm here. Please, please,' piped in Thomas.

With a grumble, the wood-carver stepped aside to let them in. He pointed to a stool near his workbench.

'No talking, no jiggling, no noise,' he ordered Thomas.

The widow McDowell handed Mr Toomey a warm loaf of corn bread as a token of thanks. Then she took out her knitting and sat down in a rocking-chair in the far corner of the cottage.

'Not there!' bellowed the wood-carver. 'No one sits in that chair.' So she moved to the straight-backed chair by the fire.

Thomas sat very still. Once, when he needed to sneeze, he pressed a finger under his nose to hold it back. Once, when he wanted desperately to scratch his leg, he counted to twenty to keep his mind off the itch.

After a very long time, Thomas cleared his throat and whispered, 'Mr Toomey, may I ask a question?'

The wood-carver glared at Thomas, then shrugged his shoulders and grunted. Thomas decided it meant 'yes', so he went on. 'Is that my sheep you're carving?'

The wood-carver nodded and grunted again.

After another very long time, Thomas whispered, 'Mr Toomey, excuse me, but you're carving my sheep wrong.'

The widow McDowell's knitting-needles stopped clicking. Jonathan Toomey's knife stopped carving. Thomas went on. 'It's a beautiful sheep, nice and curly, but my sheep looked happy.'

'That's pish-posh,' said Mr Toomey. 'Sheep are sheep. They cannot look happy.'

'Mine did,' answered Thomas. 'They knew they were with the Baby Jesus, so they were happy.'

After that, Thomas was quiet for the rest of the afternoon. When the church bells chimed six o'clock, Mr Toomey grumbled under his breath about the awful noise. The widow McDowell said it was time to leave. Thomas sneezed three times, then thanked the wood-carver for allowing him to watch.

That evening, after a supper of corn bread and boiled potatoes, the wood-carver sat down at his bench. He picked up his knife. He picked up the sheep. He worked until his eyelids drooped shut.

From *The Christmas Miracle of Jonathan Toomey*, by Susan Wojciechowski. Illustrations by P.J. Lynch. Walker Books Ltd, on behalf of Candlewick Press.

A Visit from St Nicholas

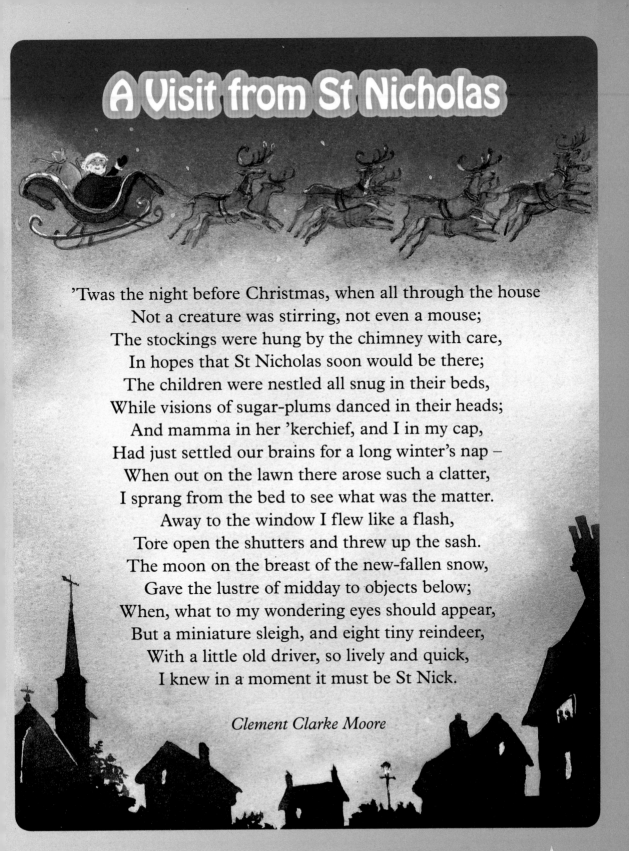

'Twas the night before Christmas, when all through the house
Not a creature was stirring, not even a mouse;
The stockings were hung by the chimney with care,
In hopes that St Nicholas soon would be there;
The children were nestled all snug in their beds,
While visions of sugar-plums danced in their heads;
And mamma in her 'kerchief, and I in my cap,
Had just settled our brains for a long winter's nap –
When out on the lawn there arose such a clatter,
I sprang from the bed to see what was the matter.
Away to the window I flew like a flash,
Tore open the shutters and threw up the sash.
The moon on the breast of the new-fallen snow,
Gave the lustre of midday to objects below;
When, what to my wondering eyes should appear,
But a miniature sleigh, and eight tiny reindeer,
With a little old driver, so lively and quick,
I knew in a moment it must be St Nick.

Clement Clarke Moore

Activities

A Let's chat

Have you ever helped someone who was sad? What made them sad? What did you do? What did you say?

B First impressions

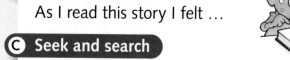

As I read this story I felt …

C Seek and search

1 What did the village children call Jonathan Toomey?
2 What did he complain about?
3 How did he spend his days?
4 Who came to his door in December? What did they want?
5 What did Thomas say to Mr Toomey about the sheep?

D Quest and query

1 What do we know about Mr Toomey that others do not?
2 What do you think the miracle will be?
3 Why do you think Mr Toomey did not want the widow to sit in the rocking chair?
4 Find as many words as you can in the story that describe Mr Toomey.
5 Why did the widow's knitting needles stop clicking?
6 Do you think Mr Toomey will make the sheep look happy? Why do you think this?

E Word watch

Antonyms are words of opposite meaning, e.g. big/small.

Find the antonyms in the following groups of words.

1 empty   pour   jug   full
2 friend   stranger   enemy   house
3 hated   brought   grumbled   liked
4 cried   laughed   complained   mumbled

Word

104

F Sounds abound

The **k** is silent in the following words: **k**nitting, **k**nife.

Unscramble the following lines to make correct sentences. Write the words that contain a silent 'k'.

1 was in village. the known Mr Toomey Mr Gloomy as
2 door. on the he knock day One heard a
3 know you are I wood-carver. a
4 took widow The McDowell her out knitting.
5 to knit. started She
6 knife. Mr Toomey out took his
7 He carve. to kneeled knee his on began and

G Watch your Ps and Qs

A **pronoun** is a small word that takes the place of a noun, e.g. you, he, she, they, I, we.

Write the following sentences and underline the pronouns.

1 He went about mumbling and grumbling.
2 The village people did not know it but he was sad.
3 'I can't remember a time without them,' she said.
4 'These are very nice wood-carvings,' he said.
5 'You won't even know I am here,' he piped up.

H Flights of fancy

You are Mr Toomey. Write a letter to widow McDowell and Thomas to thank them for showing you how to be happy again. In the first paragraph, tell them how happy they made you feel. In the next paragraph, tell them what you did over Christmas. In the last paragraph, invite them to visit you soon. Digital

I Spark starters

Find out about Christmas in China or another country.

Sheltie and the Runaway

Sally and her pony Minnow have run away. Her friend Emma and her pony Sheltie go out to search for them. They ride over the moor and through the woods, with Sheltie sniffing the air to pick up Minnow's scent.
Will they find them?

Emma squeezed her heels and Sheltie took off at a gallop. They raced down the lane to the woods behind Mr Brown's meadow. If Sally had run away, thought Emma, she would probably be heading for the open countryside, through the woods.

Emma and Sheltie took the path they always rode, the one which skirted the meadow to the woods. Emma kept a lookout for any pony tracks. Sheltie sniffed at the air, trying to pick up Minnow's scent.

The ground was hard and Emma could see no marks to show that Sally and Minnow had passed that way.

Emma and Sheltie pressed on until they came to the edge of Bramble Wood. There were several paths which led through the tangle of trees.

Sheltie pawed at the ground with his hoof and tossed his head. He wanted to take the long path which led up to higher ground. From there you could look out over the hills and down across Little Applewood. The path went up over the downs towards the main road and led on to the rolling moor.

Emma and Sheltie rode through the woods beneath the overhanging trees. At some points, the branches hung so low that Emma had to brush them out of the way with her hand.

There was no sign of Sally though until they neared the edge of the wood where the path began to rise up to higher ground.

On a branch sticking out across the path, clinging to a twig, was a clump of white horse hair. Sheltie saw it first. He stopped dead in his tracks and sniffed at the coarse hair.

It was from Minnow's mane. Sheltie had no doubt about it. He recognised the scent right away. Sheltie gave a loud snort as Emma reached out with her hand and plucked the clump of hair free.

'Clever boy, Sheltie,' said Emma. 'They must have come this way after all.' There were also a few hoof prints in the muddy track where the earth was softer. Emma squeezed with her heels and hurried Sheltie along.

'Trot on, Sheltie!'

Sheltie quickened his pace to a trot. They rode out of the wood and climbed up to the top of the downs.

There weren't so many trees here. Emma could see for miles back down over Little Applewood and beyond, across to the rolling moor. There was still no sign of Sally and Minnow though.

'Which way, Sheltie?' said Emma. Sheltie shook his long mane and sniffed the air through his nostrils. Minnow's scent was on the wind, but it was very faint.

Emma eased the reins and let Sheltie take the lead. He flicked his tail a couple of times. Then he set off over the grass across a shallow slope, heading for the moor.

An old railway line used to run through the valley on the other side of the slope between the moor and the downs. Emma could see where the railway tracks had been. The grass was thinner there and the ground was stony with gravel and rocks.

Emma and Sheltie followed the tracks until they disappeared into an abandoned tunnel that cut into the hillside. Sheltie stopped at the entrance to the tunnel and peered inside. A wooden barrier lay across the opening warning people to keep out. Sheltie made funny little snorting sounds and pawed at the ground with his hoof.

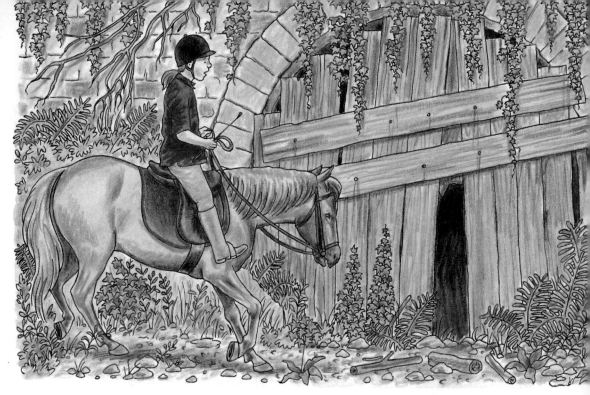

'Is it them, Sheltie?' said Emma. 'Are Sally and Minnow in there?' Sheltie nodded his head and gave a loud blow.

'Sally,' Emma called into the tunnel. 'Are you in there?' Emma's voice echoed back from inside the tunnel.

'Are you in there … there … there.' The echo faded to silence. Then Emma heard someone calling. A little voice sounding far away.

Help!
I'm in here!

'Help!'

Sheltie heard it too. His ears stood straight up.

'Sally, is that you?' Emma called again. And this time she recognised Sally's voice.

'Help! I'm in here!'

It was very dark inside the tunnel. But Emma knew Sally was in trouble, so she urged Sheltie forward.

110

Slowly they edged their way round the barrier and into the darkness. Sheltie had to be very careful. The ground was uneven where the railway tracks had been removed and there were dips and holes everywhere. Further into the tunnel, the floor became wet and slippery.

Emma saw a faint light up ahead. It was Sally. She was walking back along the tunnel towards Emma with a torch. Sally carried a small backpack and her clothes looked all wet and muddy. Emma could see that Sally had been crying. Her cheeks were wet with tears.

'Sally!' called Emma. Sally ran the last few metres to meet her friend. Emma jumped down from the saddle and gave poor Sally a big hug.

'Oh, Emma,' cried Sally. 'I'm so glad to see you! It's Minnow. He's fallen down and trapped his leg. And it's all my fault.' She began to cry again.

From *Sheltie and the Runaway*, by Peter Clover. Penguin Books.

Activities

A Let's chat

Have you ever helped friends who were in trouble? How did you help them? What did your friends say to you after you helped them?

B First impressions

I liked/disliked this story because …

C Seek and search

1 Behind who's meadow were the woods?
2 Why did Sheltie sniff the air?
3 What did they find clinging to a twig?
4 Why was there a wooden barrier at the entrance to the tunnel?
5 Why did Sheltie have to be careful in the tunnel?
6 What had happened to Minnow in the tunnel?

D Quest and query

1 Why could Emma not see pony tracks at first?
2 What do you think Little Applewood is? Explain.
3 How do you know that Sheltie has a good sense of smell?
4 Why do you think Emma squeezed Sheltie with her heels?
5 Why do you think the railway line was not being used any more?
6 Describe how Sally looked when Emma found her.

E Word watch

Complete the following sentences using the correct words from the brackets.

1 Sheltie walked carefully _____ (through/threw) the tunnel.
2 Sheltie trotted towards the rolling _____ (more/moor).
3 Emma _____ (road/rode) Sheltie to the _____ (would/wood).
4 Sheltie sniffed the _____ (air/heir) to pick up the _____ (sent/scent).
5 Emma eased the _____ (reins/rains) and he turned _____ (right/write).

F Sounds abound

Words that **rhyme** end in the same sound, e.g. but/cut. They
do not have to end in the same letters, e.g. green/mean.

Find the words in the story that rhyme with the following words.

1 pane _____   6 flowed _____

2 shadow _____   7 funnel _____

3 around _____   8 tumble _____

4 clawed _____   9 bright _____

5 line _____   10 salt _____

G Watch your Ps and Qs

An **apostrophe s** ('s) shows that something belongs to
someone, e.g. Emma's horse = The horse belonging to Emma.

Write the following sentences correctly by inserting an
apostrophe s ('s).

1 He sniffed the air trying to pick up Minnow scent.
2 Emma recognised Sally voice.
3 Sally horse was trapped in the tunnel.
4 The girl bag was on her back.
5 Emma friend had been crying.

H Flights of fancy

1 Imagine you are a reporter with a local newspaper. You are sent
   to interview Emma. Write down the questions you will ask her.
2 Write a list of things you might find in Sally's backpack.
3 Write a short summary of how Emma might rescue Sally and Minnow.

Digital

I Spark starters

Research some of the different breeds of horse using the Internet,
an encyclopaedia or your library.

From Horses to Horsepower

Horses have been very important to people for thousands of years. They have helped people to plough fields, go hunting and to pull heavy loads. They have **galloped** off into battle and gone racing for fun. Horses have done all of these things and much more. For many years, people have depended on horses and all the things they can do.

All that began to change in the late 1800s. A German called **Karl Benz** invented the modern motor car in 1885. The first car had only three wheels. It used a small petrol engine for power.

The 1885 Benz car

It did not go very fast, but people still liked it. At this time, people had to buy petrol in the chemist's shop because petrol stations did not exist. Soon, rich people all over the world wanted to own a 'horseless carriage', as the car was sometimes called.

Karl Benz

FACT BOX

Mercedes Benz cars are named after the daughter of one of Karl Benz's customers. His name was Emil Jellinek. Her name was Mercedes.

Henry Ford was an American whose father came from County Cork. In 1903, he set up the Ford Motor Company. Ford was the first person to have workers working on an **assembly line**. This meant that each worker became very skilled at a particular job. One would work on fitting doors, another on fitting seats, another on fitting windows and so on. Ford started to make cheaper cars that ordinary people could afford. His big success was the **Ford Model T** car.

The Ford Model T car

From Horses to Horsepower

Henry Ford

Its nickname was the Tin Lizzie. It was called this as it was very reliable. 'Lizzie' was a term used to describe a reliable servant. Millions of these cars were made. Soon, he was the biggest car maker in the world.

Trucks and vans were also made. As more cars, trucks and vans were made, fewer people wanted to use horses. Stables in which horses used to live became garages for cars. **Blacksmiths** who used to make shoes for horses had less work to do. Some of them became **mechanics** and looked after cars instead of horses.

Over the years, cars have become much safer, faster and more comfortable. Safety belts and airbags help prevent people getting badly hurt if there is an accident. Most cars have radios and music players. Some even have televisions, so there is no need for passengers to be bored on a long trip. There are more than one million cars in Ireland alone!

FACT BOX

A Frenchman called Nicolas Cugnot built a car that ran on steam in 1769. It had three wheels and could carry four people. It was very slow. It had to stop every 20 minutes to add more fuel and water to its boiler. Because of this, steam cars were never popular.

Cugnot's steam car

There are some very special cars that are used just for racing. They have room for only one person and can go very fast. Formula One racing cars are the fastest racing cars of all. They go so fast that mechanics have to change their tyres a few times during the race! Special races are held on race tracks all over the world.

Formula One racing car

Rally car

Rally cars are a bit more like the cars we drive around in. They are made to go extra fast. Rally cars race around on ordinary roads in the countryside. There are two people in each car, one to drive and one to tell the driver where to go.

These days, cars have engines that are cleaner and less harmful to the world around us. Cars have used petrol since the days of Karl Benz. However, the cars of the future could all be electric. Maybe you won't even have to drive your car. Just tell it where you want to go and the car will do the rest!

Activities

A **Talk about**

1 Are horses as important today as they were in the past?
2 What must you do when you are crossing the road in the following places: (a) a city, (b) a small town and (c) the countryside?
3 What do you think would happen if there were no rules of the road?

B **What have you learned?**

1 In what country was Karl Benz born?
2 What did he invent in 1885?
3 Was the 'horseless carriage' a good name for a car? Explain.
4 Before the car was invented, what work did blacksmiths do with horses?
5 Where did Karl Benz get the name Mercedes?
6 Explain what an assembly line is.
7 How did the first car differ from cars today?
8 What problems might people have had driving a car with three wheels?
9 Why do you think petrol was sold in a chemist's shop long ago?
10 Do you think the nickname 'Tin Lizzie' was a good one? Explain.

C **Think about it**

What countries are famous for manufacturing cars? Make a bar graph to show the different models of car owned by the families in your class.

D **True or false**

1 Cars were used to pull ploughs. _____
2 Henry Ford's family came to America from Cork. _____
3 At first, only rich people could afford to buy a car. _____
4 Karl Benz was Irish. _____
5 There are about 10,000 cars in Ireland. _____
6 Petrol was first sold in the butcher's shop. _____
7 Many blacksmiths became car mechanics. _____

E Complete the sentences

Rewrite this passage using the correct words from the box.

people	America	Karl	Model	rich	Tin Lizzie	car
three	ran	safer	petrol	faster	Henry	cheaper

The very first motor _____ was made by _____ Benz in 1885. It had _____ wheels. Its engine _____ on _____. At first, only very _____ people could own a car. That all changed when _____ Ford began to make _____ cars in _____. The Ford _____ T was a real success and lots of _____ bought it. This car was also called the _____ _____. Over the years, cars have become _____ and _____.

F Word connections

Find the five words connected with cars in the word box.
Put each word into a sentence.

tyre	paddle	rope	windscreen	gears
oars	deck	brakes	headlights	sail

What do all the other words have in common?

G Look it up

Use an encyclopaedia or the Internet to answer the following questions.

1 What is the maximum speed limit on:
   (a) motorways and (b) national roads in Ireland?
2 What is the world land speed record?

H Write about it

1 What clever things would you like your future car to do?
2 Draw a picture of your dream car and write about it.

When Jessie Came Across the Sea

Jessie lives with her grandmother. Life is very simple, but happy. One day, the village rabbi receives a ticket to America, the land of wealth and opportunity. Who will he choose to give the ticket to?

Once, in a poor village far from here, there was a very small house with a slanting roof. Inside were two chairs, two narrow beds, and a table with a fine lace cloth. A potbellied stove warmed the place in winter, and warmed thin soup.

Jessie lived in that house with Grandmother. They had one skinny cow – Miss Minnie – and a patch of garden. Carrots came up here and there, and sometimes a potato.

Long ago, when Jessie was a baby, her parents died. Jessie kept her mother's wedding ring, though, in a tiny silver box with a tiny lace lining. From time to time she tried it on.

In the morning, when the village boys went to the rabbi for lessons, Jessie went too. Grandmother insisted. At night, after supper, Jessie read out loud. She practised her letters by the fire. Grandmother sewed lace. The coins she earned were dropped in a jar on the table.

'Now, you read, Grandmother, and copy my good letters.' Jessie liked being teacher.

'Me? Learn to read and write?' Grandmother scoffed.

'Sometime, you never know, you may want to read some things,' Jessie said. 'You may want to write.'

Grandmother showed Jessie how to sew lace.

But Jessie pricked herself often. 'Why do I have to learn?' she cried.

'Sometime, you never know, you may want to sew some things,' Grandmother answered. 'You may want to earn some money.'

One evening, towards the end of
summer, the rabbi called the people
of the village to the synagogue.
'The news from America is sad,'
said the rabbi. 'My good brother,
Mordecai, has left this world.'

The villagers sighed and shook
their heads. 'Rest in peace,' they said.

'Shortly before he died, my Mordecai sent me a ticket to America.' The rabbi paused. 'He wanted me to join him there.'

'America! The promised land!' The voices rose as one.

'But alas!' The rabbi sighed. 'I am the rabbi. How can I leave this village? How can I abandon my people?' He threw up his hands. 'Someone else must go in my place, someone of my choosing.'

Later that night, many villagers came to the rabbi's house.

'Rabbi, listen to reason! I must go to America, for I am strong!'

'Rabbi, listen to good sense! I must go to America, for I am smart!'

'Rabbi, listen to logic! I must go to America, for I am brave!'

The rabbi listened. *How they boast and brag!* he thought. 'Tonight I shall seek guidance from the Almighty,' he told the villagers. 'You go home. Tomorrow I will choose.'

Early the next morning, Jessie and Grandmother had a caller. 'I have decided,' announced the rabbi. 'Jessie will go to America. My brother's widow has a dress shop

in New York City. Her name is Kay, and Jessie can help with the sewing. She will comfort the good lady.'

Jessie's hands started to shake. *America? So far away from Grandmother!* She bit her lip, for she must not cry in front of the rabbi. *Don't make me go!* she thought.

'You know best.' Grandmother spoke quietly to the rabbi. Oh, but her heart was breaking! *Dear Jessie, alone on a ship to America!* Grandmother's heart said one thing, but her head said another. Jessie must go.

From *When Jessie Came Across the Sea*, by Amy Hest.
Illustrations by P.J. Lynch. Walker Books Ltd.

The Sound Collector

A stranger called this morning
Dressed all in black and grey.
Put every sound into a bag
And carried them away.

The whistling of the kettle
The turning of the lock
The purring of the kitten
The ticking of the clock.

The popping of the toaster
The crunching of the flakes
When you spread the marmalade
The scraping noise it makes.

The hissing of the frying-pan
The ticking of the grill
The bubbling of the bathtub
As it starts to fill.

The drumming of the raindrops
On the window pane
When you do the washing up
The gurgle of the drain.

The crying of the baby
The squeaking of the chair
The swishing of the curtain
The creaking of the chair.

A stranger called this morning
He didn't leave his name
Left us only silence
Life will never be the same.

Roger McGough

Activities

A Let's chat

Have you ever travelled to another country? How did you
get there? What happened on the way? How did you feel?

B First impressions

I felt sorry for …

C Seek and search

1 With whom did Jessie live?
2 Where did Jessie keep her mother's wedding ring?
3 Who taught Jessie and the village boys their lessons?
4 To where did the rabbi call the people of the village?
5 Who did the rabbi choose to go to America?

D Quest and query

1 Why do you think only the village boys went to the rabbi for lessons?
2 What did the rabbi mean by 'How they boast and brag'?
3 Do you think Jessie wanted to go to America? Explain.
4 How did the rabbi decide who should go to America?
5 Why would a person emigrate, leaving everything they
   know, to start a new life in a strange place?

E Word watch

Words are arranged in alphabetical order in a dictionary.

a b c d e f g h i j k l m n o p q r s t u v w x y z

Write each of the following lists of words in alphabetical order.

1 join, stove, winter, carrots, garden
2 lace, rabbi, synagogue, another, village
3 strong, widow, heart, garden, people
4 ship, head, abandon, money, fire
5 read, write, sew, teacher, cloth

Word

F Watch your Ps and Qs

Choose the correct verb to complete the sentences.

was/were

1 In the village there _____ a very small house.

2 Jessie and her grandmother _____ very poor.

3 The coins she earned _____ dropped into a jar.

4 The villagers _____ boasting and bragging.

5 Jessie _____ chosen to go to America.

is/are

1 It _____ important to be able to read and write.

2 We _____ going to the synagogue.

3 America _____ very far away.

4 We _____ travelling by ship.

5 The Statue of Liberty _____ in America.

G Flights of fancy

Write an ending for this story. Use some of the words below.

> week passed; journey; huge ship; nervous and excited;
> passengers; hustle and bustle; crammed; ill; alone;
> dreams of America; sewing lace; swapped stories;
> Statue of Liberty; New York City; docked at Ellis Island;
> papers checked; cousin Kay; work; grandmother

Digital

H Spark starters

Find out about emigrants going to America years ago.
What was life on the ships like? What sights would they
have seen when they reached America? What work would
they have done there?

War Game

This story takes place in the middle of World War 1,
in war-torn France. One Christmas Day, an extraordinary
thing happened. British and German soldiers, enemies
at war, came out of their trenches one by one to play an
historic game of football in No Man's Land. This was an
area of land between the trenches that no man could
enter without fear of being shot.

At dawn, when the British were all 'Stood To' on the fire-step, they saw a world white with frost. The few shattered trees that remained were white. Lines of wire glinted like tinsel. The humps of dead in No Man's Land were like toppled snowmen.

After the singing of the night, the Christmas dawn was strangely quiet. The clock of death had stopped ticking.

Then a German climbed from his trench and planted a Christmas tree in No Man's Land. Freddie, being a goalkeeper and therefore a bit daft, walked out and shook hands with him. Both sides applauded.

A small group of men from each side, unarmed, joined them. They all shook hands. One of the Germans spoke good English and said he hoped the war would end soon because he wanted to return to his job as a taxi driver in Birmingham.

It was agreed that they should take the opportunity to bury the dead. The bodies were mixed up together.

They were sorted out, and a joint burial service was held on the 'halfway line'.

Both sides then returned to their trenches for breakfast. Will and the lads were cheered by the wonderful smell of bacon, and they had a hot breakfast for a change.

One by one, birds began to arrive from all sides. The soldiers hardly ever saw a bird normally, but Will counted at least fifty sparrows hopping around their trench.

Christmas presents for the men consisted of a packet of chocolate, Oxo cubes, a khaki handkerchief, peppermints, camp cocoa, writing paper and a pencil. After breakfast a pair of horses and a wagon arrived with Princess Mary's Christmas gifts – a pipe and tobacco and a Christmas card from the King and Queen.

There were no planes overhead, no observation balloons, no bombs, no rifle fire, no snipers, just an occasional skylark. The early mist lifted to reveal a clear blue sky. The Germans were strolling about on their parapet once more, and waved to the British to join them. Soon there was quite a crowd in No Man's Land. Both sides exchanged small gifts.

One German had been a barber in Holborn in London. A chair was placed on the 'halfway line', and he gave haircuts to several of the British soldiers.

Then, from somewhere, a football bounced across the frozen mud. Will was on it in a flash. He trapped the ball with his left foot, flipped it up with his right, and headed it towards Freddie.

Freddie made a spectacular dive, caught the ball in both hands and threw it to a group of Germans.

Immediately a vast, fast and furious football match was under way. Goals were marked by caps. Freddie, of course, was in one goal and a huge German in the other.

Apart from that, it was wonderfully disorganised, part football, part ice-skating, with unknown numbers on each team. No referee, no account of the score.

It was just terrific to be no longer an army of moles, but up and running on top of the ground that had threatened to entomb them for so long. And this time Will really could hear a big crowd – and he was playing for England!

He was playing in his usual centre forward position with Lacey to his left and little Billy on the wing.

The game surged back and forth across No Man's Land. The goalposts grew larger as greatcoats and tunics were discarded as the players warmed to the sport. Khaki and grey mixed together. Steam rose from their backs, and their faces were wreathed in smiles and clouds of breath in the clear frosty air.

Some of the British officers took a dim view of such sport, and when the game came to its exhausted end, the men were encouraged back to their trenches for a carol service and supper. The haunting sound of men singing drifted back and forth across No Man's Land in the still night air.

'Good night, Tommies. See you tomorrow.'

'Good night, Fritz. We'll have another game.'

From *War Game*, by Michael Foreman. Anova Books.

Activities

A Let's chat

When did World War 1 take place? Name some countries that
were involved. List some words that are associated with war.

B First impressions

As I read this story, I felt …

C Seek and search

1 Who planted a Christmas tree in No Man's Land?
2 Where was the joint burial service held?
3 What Christmas presents did the men receive?
4 Name the four friends in the story.
5 Where did the men go after the football game?

D Quest and query

1 What do you think the author means by 'the clock of death
   had stopped ticking'?
2 Why do you think the bodies were mixed up together?
3 How do you know the men were happy playing football?
4 Do you think they had another game the next day? Explain.
5 Why did Freddie feel they were 'no longer an army of moles'?

E Word watch

Choose the word(s) closest in meaning to the underlined word.

1 Both sides <u>applauded</u> each other.
   (a) shook hands, (b) clapped, (c) waved, (d) smiled
2 Freddie made a <u>spectacular</u> dive.
   (a) big, (b) visually striking, (c) quick, (d) huge
3 The players <u>discarded</u> their greatcoats and tunics.
   (a) threw off, (b) put on, (c) wore, (d) lifted
4 The game came to its <u>exhausted</u> end.
   (a) quick, (b) tired, (c) slow, (d) final

F Watch your Ps and Qs

If a verb ends in **e**, simply add **d** to make the past tense, e.g. hope/hoped.
If a verb ends in a single consonant, with a single vowel before it, double the
last letter before adding **ed** to make the past tense, e.g. trap/trapped.

Write the past tense of the following words.

(a) bounce	(b) flip	(c) topple	(d) drop	(e) drag
(f) stop	(g) arrive	(h) rub	(i) place	(j) hope

G Sounds abound

Sometimes **g** has a hard sound, e.g. game. At other times, **g** has a soft sound
like the letter **j**, e.g. German. The **g** is usually soft when followed by the
letters **e**, **i** or **y**.

1 Write each of the following words under the heading **Soft g** or **Hard g**.

game	Germans	groups	goals	gifts	danger
good	gasping	giant	gentle	magic	glassy

2 Use a word from the box above to complete the following sentences.

(a) The soldiers stood around in _____ .

(b) Caps were used to mark _____ .

(c) The opposite of bad is _____ .

(d) The soldiers received Christmas _____ .

H Flights of fancy

Imagine you are Freddie. Write a letter to your family telling
them about the football match. **Digital**

I Spark starters

Find out about conditions in the trenches in
World War 1 in terms of food, nutrition etc.

Vikings

The **Norse** people lived in the cold lands in the north of Europe. They had long, dark winters and short, bright summers. It was a hard place in which to make a living. It had marshes, dark forests, high rocky mountains and cold stormy seas.

A Norwegian mountain

FACT BOX

The Norse people lived in an area that we now call Norway, Denmark and Sweden. These countries make up most of Scandinavia.

The Norse people often found it easier to travel by sea than over high mountains or through dark forests. They learned how to build strong boats and ships. Many became great sailors. They would fish and trade in their well made boats. They also learned how to get iron from rocks. They made tools and weapons with the iron.

Some of the Norse people did not want to be farmers, builders or fishermen. Instead, they became invaders! They would sail in their strong ships and **raid** other places, taking what they wanted. The Norse saying for this was to 'go a-Viking'. Any Norse man who became an invader was called a **Viking**.

A Viking helmet

A Viking axe

More than a thousand years ago, the Vikings were the most feared people in Europe. Many of them were vicious. They dressed in frightening clothes. They used swords and axes to kill people.

Vikings were thought to be the best sailors around at that time. They had the best ships. Viking **longships** were beautiful: sleek, strong and fast. Every man on board helped to row the ship with long **oars**. The longship also had a high sail to catch the wind. This meant that the men could have a rest when the wind blew. The front of the longship often had a monster's head carved onto it to make it look even more scary.

A Viking longship replica

The longships could travel far and fast. Vikings could row one up a river or straight onto a beach. They could then attack a village or a monastery. Vikings were always looking for gold and silver to steal. The monasteries had lots of gold and silver religious ornaments. To try to stop the Vikings, some monks built high **round towers** at the monasteries. From the top of these towers, they could see the Vikings coming. This gave them time to hide the precious items high in the towers, where they were safe from the Vikings.

The first Viking raiders came to Ireland from Norway in about 795 AD. It was their first attack in Ireland. Unfortunately, it would not be their last. In the years that followed, there would be many more Viking raids. They decided to set up camps in Ireland, where they could stay. They would use the camps as bases from which to make their attacks.

FACT BOX

The Vikings travelled as far as Africa and America. It is thought that they even reached America about 500 years before **Christopher Columbus** did.

There was one big problem for the Vikings in Ireland. The ordinary Irish people in villages did not use gold or silver for money. Instead, they used a system called **barter**. If they had potatoes and wanted to buy chickens, they found a farmer who was prepared to swap. That was no good for the Vikings. They wanted money, not chickens, cows or pigs.

The Irish monasteries were good places for raiding, but the villages were not as good. However, Ireland was a very good place for farming. Other Norse people heard about Ireland from the Vikings. They wanted to farm on this land. Many Norse people came to live in the Viking camps in Ireland. They turned the Viking camps into places where people traded goods and made things. Some of these camps grew into towns such as Dublin, Wexford, Waterford and Cork.

A round tower in an ancient Irish monastery

FACT BOX

Norse traders used a slower, bigger ship than a longship. It was called a **knorr**. It could carry a lot of **cargo**.

Activities

A **Talk about**

Would you like to have been alive around the time of the Vikings?
Give reasons for your answer. What would life have been like?

B **What have you learned?**

1 From where did the Norse people come?
2 Why do you think they found it easier to travel by sea?
3 What was an invading Norseman called?
4 Why did the Vikings dress in frightening clothes?
5 What kind of ships did the Vikings use?
6 Who preferred to use ships called knorrs?
7 When did the Vikings first attack Ireland?
8 Name four towns or cities in Ireland that the Vikings helped to build.
9 Do you think barter was a good system of trade? Why?
10 How do you think Ireland benefited from the Vikings?

C **True or false**

1 A Viking longship could travel far and fast. _____
2 The Vikings had horns on their helmets. _____
3 The first Vikings came to Ireland in about 795 AD. _____
4 Barter is still used in Ireland for trade. _____
5 Vikings loved gold and silver. _____
6 Norse traders used big ships called knorrs. _____

D **Mixed-up sentences**

Sort out the following mixed-up sentences.

1 Ireland sailed Vikings to on longships.
2 lived in Scandinavia. people The Norse
3 tools Vikings and weapons made with iron.
4 monasteries The gold. of lots had
5 could of cargo. A knorr carry a lot

E **Complete the sentences**

Rewrite this passage using the correct words from the box.

sail	monster	river	scary	helmets
Vikings	fast	swords	jump	way

Viking longships were very _____. They could sail a very long _____.
The _____ could use oars or the wind to make it _____. They could even
sail up a _____ if they wanted to. The longship had a scary _____ head
on the front. When the Vikings got to a place they wanted to raid, they
would _____ out of their longship and attack. They had _____ and axes.
They wore _____ on their heads. They were a very _____ group of people.

F **Draw a picture**

Draw a Viking longship in your copy.

G **Look it up**

Use your library or the Internet to answer the following questions.

1 What food did the Vikings like to eat?
2 What were the names of the main Viking gods?
3 Famous men from the era of the Vikings are Eric the Red and Leif Eriksson.
   Find out as much as you can about these men.

H **Finish the story**

You are sitting beside a river early one morning long ago. With your
fishing rod in your hand, you are hoping to catch a fish. There is
still a mist on the river. Just then, out of the mist, you see first the
monster's head and then the rest of a longship. The Vikings are
coming! You have to warn people in your village …

Gulliver's Travels

The little boat in which Lemuel Gulliver is sailing gets wrecked in a terrible storm. Tired out after swimming ashore, he lies down on the short, soft grass and goes to sleep. After some time, he wakes up to find himself tied firmly to the ground. He is surrounded by thousands of little men. Who are these little people? How did they manage to tie him down? What will happen to him?

My travels began on May 4th 1699. I said goodbye to my wife and two children and set sail from Bristol as ship's doctor bound for the South Seas.

All went well for the first few weeks. Then there was
a bad storm and the ship was wrecked. Six of the crew,
of whom I was one, got into a little boat and began to row
to an island nearby. Suddenly a huge wave upset the boat,
and all the other men were lost. Only I, Lemuel Gulliver,
was left.

I swam as long as I could and at last, just as I could
swim no more, my feet touched the bottom. I waded
through the water to the shore, where there was no sign of
houses or people.

I walked about half a mile further, but still saw no one.
Tired out, I lay down on the short, soft grass and went
to sleep.

When I woke up it was daylight. I lay still for a moment wondering where I was, then tried to get up. I could not move my arms or my legs or my head! I was tied to the ground! There was a buzzing noise near me but I could not see what was making it.

Suddenly I felt something moving on my left leg. It walked up me and stopped close by my chin. I looked down as well as I could (for my hair was tied to the ground), and saw a tiny man, less than six inches high, with a bow and arrow in his hand. Then many more of these little men started to run all over me. I was so surprised that I roared loudly.

They ran back in a fright and fell over one another trying to get away. I found out later that some of them had hurt themselves when they fell from my chest.

I managed to break the strings that tied my left arm to the ground, and pulled some of my hair loose so that I could move my head. This made the little men even more afraid, and they shot arrows at me. Some fell on my hands and some on my face, pricking me like needles and making my skin sore wherever they landed.

The little men stood around at a distance watching me. After a while, when they saw I was not going to hurt them, they cut some of the strings that bound me. This at least allowed me to move my head more.

Now I could see that they had built a little platform beside my head so that their emperor could talk to me. He spoke for some time, but I could not understand him, and I began to grow hungry. I pointed to my mouth and pretended to chew. He seemed to understand and at once sent some of his men to bring me food and drink.

Ladders were put against my sides, and over a hundred of the little men climbed up, bringing baskets full of meat and bread. Each piece of meat was the size of one small piece of mince, so I had to keep asking for more. The loaves were so tiny that I ate three at a time.

I drank a whole barrel of their wine at a gulp. They kept looking at each other as if they could not believe it was possible to drink so much, but they brought me some more wine which I drank.

I made signs to let them know I would not try to escape, and they loosened the strings so that I could turn on my side. They also put some ointment on my face and hands, which took away the soreness their arrows had caused.

Then I fell asleep again.

From *Gulliver's Travels*, by Jonathan Swift.
Penguin Books Ltd.

NOISES IN THE NIGHT

What's that scratching
at the window-pane?
Who's that knocking
again and again?
What's that creeping
across the floor?
And who's that tapping
at my bedroom door?

What's that creaking
beneath my bed?
Who's that walking
with a slow tread?
What's that whirring
in the air?
And who's that coming
up the squeaky stair?

I lie in bed
and I'm wide awake.
The noises make me
shiver and shake.
But soon all's quiet
and the dark is deep.
So I close my eyes
and fall a…

Wes Magee

Activities

A Let's chat

Imagine that you have travelled to a strange or fantasy land. Where would this be? Who would live there? What wonderful things would happen on your travels?

B First impressions

As I read I wondered why …

C Seek and search

1 In what year did Gulliver's travels begin?
2 What happened to Gulliver's companions?
3 Why could Gulliver not get up when he awoke?
4 What did the little men put up against his sides?
5 What did they put on Gulliver's face and hands? Why?

D Quest and query

1 Why might Gulliver have thought the island was deserted?
2 How do you know the little men were afraid of Gulliver?
3 What do you think the emperor said to Gulliver?
4 How did Gulliver show that he was hungry?
5 How do you know that the loaves were small?
6 How did the little men show that they were kind/gentle?

E Word watch

Complete the following word groups using words from the story.

1 family, brood, offspring, _____

2 vessel, boat, craft, liner, _____

3 dart, shot, needle, projectile, _____

4 stage, raised area, stand, podium, _____

5 starving, famished, ravenous, _____

6 cream, gel, lotion, balm, _____

Word

F Sounds abound

Make a word from the story by changing the first letter of each of the following words, e.g. poke/woke.

1 save   **2** there   **3** calf   **4** would   **5** sigh

6 soared   **7** round   **8** south   **9** wince   **10** paused

G Watch your Ps and Qs

An **adjective** is a describing word. It describes a noun, e.g. A **huge** wave upset the **small, yellow** boat.

Write down the adjectives from the following sentences.

1 I lay down on the short, soft grass and went to sleep.
2 There was a loud, buzzing noise near me.
3 The little men fired sharp arrows at me.
4 I broke the thin strings that tied my left arm to the ground.
5 They put ointment on my sore face and bleeding hands.

H Flights of fancy

A story has a **beginning**, a **middle** and an **ending**.

Imagine you are Gulliver. You land on an island of giants. Write about your adventure using the following headings.

Beginning: Decide on your setting, e.g. beach, jungle. Describe the main character/minor characters.
Middle: Describe the problem – you are shipwrecked/lost.
Ending: How will the problem be resolved? Digital

I Spark starters

Find out about some famous shipwrecks, e.g. the *Titanic*, the *Andrea Doria*, the *Mary Rose*, the *General Slocum* and the *Lusitania*.

Oisín

Fionn and his hounds Bran and Sceolán are returning home after a day of hunting. Suddenly, a beautiful fawn appears in front of them. The hounds chase the fawn and then lie down beside her. That night, a beautiful woman appears at Fionn's bedside. She tells Fionn that her name is Sadhb (*si-ve*) and that a druid called the Fear Dorcha wanted her to become his wife. When she refused, he cast a spell on her, turning her into a fawn. Would Fionn, her true love, be able to protect her and save her from the Fear Dorcha?

It was evening and Fionn was returning home. His two hounds Bran and Sceolán were at his side. Suddenly, a fawn jumped out in front of them and immediately the hounds gave chase. Fionn followed and, to his great surprise, when he finally caught up with them, the hounds were lying peacefully beside the fawn.

'She must be one of the Fairy people,' he thought
to himself.

During the night, Fionn woke to find a beautiful young
girl standing at his bedside. He knew that she must be the
fawn he had hunted that day.

'I need your help, Fionn,' she whispered softly.
'My name is Sadhb, and you are the only one who can
help me. Two years ago, one of the druids of my people,
the Fear Dorcha, wanted me to be his wife. When I
refused, he cast a spell on me and turned me into a fawn.
Only the man I love can protect me.'

'Tell me where he is and I will take you to him,'
Fionn answered.

'He is here in front of me,' cried Sadhb. 'While I am
with you I can take human form and the Fear Dorcha
cannot harm me.'

Fionn was delighted to hear this, for he had fallen in
love with Sadhb as soon as he had seen her.

Within a short time they were married and they lived happily in his fort on the Hill of Allen.

One day Fionn received news that the Norsemen were coming again, in their longships, to attack. Fionn prepared to leave at once. It was the duty of the Fianna to protect the country from any invaders.

Before leaving he warned Sadhb not to venture outside the fort until he returned.

The fight was long and difficult, but eventually the invaders were driven back to their ships. Immediately, Fionn set off for home.

As Fionn approached the fort he was troubled. He could see no sign of Sadhb coming to greet him. Then he grew fearful and rushed into the fort.

His chief steward came to him and told him terrible news. 'One morning as Sadhb looked over the plain, she gave a great shout of joy. She cried out that you were returning. We looked out and we saw you with Bran and Sceolán, but were surprised that none of your warriors were with you. Before anyone could say a word, Sadhb ran out to welcome you home.'

'As she drew near you, she realised that it wasn't you, but the Fear Dorcha. We were powerless, and could only watch helplessly as he touched her with a hazel rod and she became a fawn. She tried to escape but his two hounds prevented her. There was nothing we could do!'

Fionn spent the next seven years searching for Sadhb, but with no success. One evening, as he was returning home, his two hounds suddenly raced off in the direction of a small wood. Fionn was overcome by a strange feeling, and followed them curiously.

There, under a tree, was a little boy of about seven years old. The boy and Fionn looked at each other. Then the little boy reached out his hand and placed it in Fionn's. Fionn looked into the boy's face and recognised the eyes of his beautiful wife, Sadhb. He knew that this was his son.

The little boy returned home with Fionn. At first he could not speak, but gradually, as he learnt the language, he told Fionn about the fawn that had taken care of him.

He spoke about a tall, dark man who would appear and try to talk to the fawn, but she would always run away. The last thing he remembered before meeting Fionn was the dark man hitting the fawn with a hazel rod and forcing her to follow him.

'You are indeed my son,' said Fionn sadly. 'I loved your mother, but the Fear Dorcha stole her from me. He has no power over you. You will stay with me and when you are old enough you will join the Fianna. I will call you Oisín, Little Fawn.'

Oisín became a great warrior and a famous poet.
When he grew up, he visited his mother in Tír na n-Óg.

Oisín. From *Irish Legends for Children,* by Yvonne Carroll. Gill & Macmillan.

Activities

A Let's chat

Would you like to have lived in Ireland during the time of Oisín? How would your life be different?

B First impressions

I would like to know …

C Seek and search

1 Name Fionn's two hounds.
2 What suddenly jumped out in front of them?
3 Who turned Sadhb into a fawn?
4 In what did the Norsemen come across the sea?
5 What name did Fionn give his son?

D Quest and query

1 Why did Fionn think the fawn was one of the fairy people?
2 Why do you think the Fear Dorcha got this name?
3 How did the Fear Dorcha trick Sadhb?
4 Where did he take her? How do you know this?
5 How do you think Fionn felt when (a) he returned home to find that Sadhb was gone, and (b) he found his son in the forest?

E Word watch

Homophones are words that sound the same but have a different spelling and meaning, e.g. Fionn was a great/grate hunter.

Write the following sentences using the correct homophone.

1 He new/knew she must be the fawn he had hunted.
2 Sadhb looked over the plain/plane.
3 The two/to hounds prevented her from escaping.
4 There, under a tree/three, was a little boy/buoy.
5 Oisín was Fionn's son/sun.

Word

F Sounds abound

-ight at the end of words usually sounds like **ite**, e.g. ni**ght**.
Match each of the following **-ight** words to its meaning.

delight	battle		flight	two weeks
right	joy		fortnight	opposite of day
fight	correct		night	opposite of dark
fright	fear		light	escape

G Watch your Ps and Qs

An **adverb** describes a verb. Adverbs usually end in **ly**.

1 Change the following adjectives into adverbs,
   e.g. peaceful/peacefully.

(a) immediate (b) soft (c) eventual (d) fearful (e) helpless
(f) curious (g) sad (h) gradual (i) bad (j) sorrowful

If an **adjective** ends with **y**, change the **y** to **ily** to make the adverb,
e.g. happy/happily.

2 Change the following adjectives into adverbs.

(a) angry (b) busy (c) lucky (d) merry (e) pretty

H Flights of fancy

Write the following sentences in the correct order to retell the story.

1 Fionn married Sadhb and they lived happily.
2 Fionn left as the Norsemen had arrived in the country.
3 That night, a beautiful woman appeared to Fionn.
4 Fionn and his hounds were returning home when they
   saw a fawn.
5 Fionn searched for Sadhb but could not find her.
6 The Fear Dorcha changed Sadhb into a fawn again.

Hurling

Hurling is one of the oldest, and probably the fastest, field games in the world. The **Celts** came to Ireland from mainland Europe about 3,000 years ago. They brought with them their own music, language and pastimes. One of these pastimes was the game of hurling. Hurling is quite like the game of 'shinty', which is still played in Scotland today.

   Irish warriors, like Cú Chulainn and Fionn MacCumhaill, are thought to have played hurling. An old legend tells us how Setanta got the name Cú Chulainn. Setanta was invited to a feast at the house of Culann. His uncle, Conor Mac Neasa, called to his house to bring him to the feast. Setanta was in the middle of a game of hurling. He told his uncle that he would follow him to the feast when the game was over. Later that evening, Setanta came to the gate of Culann's house. He was attacked by Culann's guard dog. He thought that he was going to die. He hit the sliotar (hurling ball) with his camán and killed the dog. Culann had heard the dog barking and ran to the gate. He looked sadly at his dead dog. Setanta said that he would take the place of his guard dog.

FACT BOX

Sliotars are a little bigger than tennis balls. They are usually handmade from cork covered with two pieces of leather that are stitched together.

From then on, he was called Cú Chulainn. This means 'the hound of Culann'.

   The first hurling matches were probably played between villages, to settle rows or just for fun. Hundreds of people played on each team. The games went on for hours, even days!

FACT BOX

Camáns (hurley sticks) are carved out of wood from the ash tree. The wood is dried, sanded and shaped by master craftsmen. Linseed oil should be rubbed into a *camán* regularly to prevent it from drying out and splitting.

Camogie is the name of the popular hurling game played by girls and women.

Nowadays, most hurling games last 70 minutes. There are 15 players on each team. The goalposts have a crossbar. A goal is worth three points. A goal is scored by hitting the sliotar under the bar into the net. A point is scored by hitting the sliotar over the bar.

Most towns and villages in Ireland have a hurling team. It is a great honour to play for your county. Every September, the All-Ireland Championship Final is played in Croke Park in Dublin. The winning team brings home the McCarthy Cup. Every county would love to win the All-Ireland Championship. The most successful teams in recent years have been Kilkenny, Tipperary and Cork. However, Wexford, Waterford, Clare, Galway, Limerick, Dublin and Offaly have also had great hurling teams.

The *poc fada* (long puck) is a competition that is held every year in the Cooley Mountains in County Louth. The winner is the person who takes the least number of 'pucks' (hits) of a sliotar to complete a 5-kilometre course.

Hurling is an **amateur** sport. This means that the players do not get paid for playing the game. They play for pride, and they train for many hours every week. Hurling is a great Irish game that needs skill and speed, a good aim and a good catch. If you have these skills, maybe one day you will pull on your county jersey and run onto the pitch in Croke Park to the deafening roar of more than 80,000 fans!

Helmet and faceguard: hurling can be quite dangerous if you do not wear protection. All hurling players must now wear a helmet for their safety. People who do not wear a helmet are not allowed to play.

Activities

A ❲Talk about❳

1 Talk about a hurling/camogie game you have seen.
2 Why should people start to play hurling/camogie when they are young?

B ❲What have you learned?❳

1 Who first brought the game of hurling to Ireland?
2 What Scottish game is quite like hurling?
3 From what trees are *camáns* made?
4 How did Cú Chulainn get his name?
5 How do you think Cú Chulainn felt when he saw that the dog was dead?
6 How many players are there on a hurling team nowadays?
7 What do you think it was like to play hurling with 100 people on each team?
8 How long is the *poc fada* course?
9 In what county are the Cooley Mountains?
10 Explain why it is always necessary to wear head gear when playing hurling.

C ❲Name the county❳

| 1 | 2 | 3 | 4 | 5 |

| 6 | 7 | 8 | 9 | 10 |

D Complete the sentences

Rewrite this passage using the correct words from the box.

McCarthy	Celts	minutes	shinty	goal
Ireland	village	days	fifteen	guard
sliotar	point	Croke	helmet	September

The _____ first introduced hurling to Ireland. They play a game like it called _____ in Scotland. Long ago one _____ would play another. These games could last for _____. Nowadays, most hurling games last for 70 _____.

There are _____ players on each team. Players must wear a _____ and a face _____ for protection. A _____ is scored when the _____ is hit into the net. A _____ is scored when the *sliotar* is hit over the bar. The final of the All-_____ Championship is held in _____ Park every _____.

The winners take home the _____ Cup.

E Look it up

Use the Internet to help you answer the following questions.

1 Which team won the McCarthy Cup last September?
2 Which county has won the most All-Ireland Senior Hurling Championships?
3 Find out as much as you can about Liam McCarthy.

F Finish the story

As I ran out onto the field, the crowd roared and waved their flags and banners. The big day had come and I was about to play in my first All-Ireland Championship Final. Never before had I felt so proud to be wearing my county's colours.

The Carpet Bicycle

Class Three have just returned to school after the Christmas holidays. Everyone is in a bad mood. Even the head teacher Mr Potter is cross. The new teacher has not arrived. Suddenly, in through a window flies a man on a magic carpet. Who could this man be?

It was Monday morning, it was pouring with rain, and it was everyone's first day back at St Barty's Primary School after the Christmas holidays. That's why Class Three were in a bad temper.

Pandora Green had been rude to Melanie, so Melanie was crying (though Melanie always found *something* to cry about). Hamish Bigmore was trying to pick a quarrel with Thomas and Pete, the twins. And Mr Potter the head teacher was very cross because the new teacher for Class Three hadn't turned up.

'I can't think where he is,' he grumbled at Class Three. 'He should have been here at nine o'clock for the beginning of school. And now it's nearly ten, and I should be teaching Class Two. We'll have to open the folding doors and let you share the lesson with them.'

Class Three groaned. They thought themselves very important people, and didn't in the least want to share a lesson with Class Two, who were just babies.

'Bother this thing,' muttered Mr Potter, struggling with the folding doors that separated the classrooms.

'*I'll* help you, Mr Potter,' said Hamish Bigmore, who didn't really want to help at all, but just to be a nuisance as usual. And then everyone else began to shout: 'Don't let Hamish Bigmore do it, he's no good, let *me* help,' so that in a moment there was uproar.

But suddenly silence fell. And there was a gasp.

Mr Potter was still fiddling with the folding doors, so he didn't see what was happening. But Class Three did.

One of the big windows in the classroom slid open all by itself, and *something* flew in.

It was a man on a magic carpet.

There could be no doubt about that. Class Three knew a magic carpet when they saw one. After all, they'd read *Aladdin* and all that sort of stuff. There are magic carpets all over the place in *Aladdin*. But this wasn't *Aladdin*. This was St Barty's Primary School on a wet Monday morning. And magic carpets don't turn up in schools. Class Three knew that. So they stared.

The carpet hung in the air for a moment, as if it wasn't sure what to do. Then it came down on the floor with a bump. 'Ow!' said the man sitting on it.

He was quite old, and he had a pointed beard and very bright eyes, behind a pair of glasses. His hair and clothes were wet from the rain. On the whole he looked quite ordinary – except for the fact that he was sitting on a magic carpet.

'I just can't manage it,' said Mr Potter, still pushing at the folding doors. 'I'll have to go and get the caretaker.'

Then he saw the man on the carpet.

'What – how – eh?' said Mr Potter. Words usually deserted Mr Potter at difficult moments.

The man on the carpet scrambled to his feet. 'Majeika,' he said politely, offering his hand.

Mr Potter took the hand. 'Majeika?' he repeated, puzzled. Then a look of understanding dawned on his face. 'Ah,' he said, 'Mr Majeika!' He turned to Class Three. 'Boys and girls,' he said, 'I want you to meet Mr Majeika. He's your new teacher.'

For a moment there was silence. Then Melanie began to cry: 'Boo-hoo! I'm *frightened* of him! He came on a magic carpet!'

'What's the matter, Melanie?' snapped Mr Potter. 'I can't hear a word you're saying. It sounded like "magic carpet" or some such nonsense.' He turned briskly to Mr Majeika. 'Now, you're rather late, Mr Majeika. You might have telephoned me.'

'I'm so sorry,' said Mr Majeika. 'You see, my magic carpet took a wrong turning. It's normally quite good at finding the way, but I think the rain must have got into it. I do beg your pardon.'

'Never mind,' said Mr Potter. 'And now … Wait a minute, did I hear you say *magic carpet*?'

It was Mr Majeika's turn to look bothered. 'Oh, did I really say that? How very silly of me. A complete slip of the tongue. I meant – *bicycle*, of course. I came on a bicycle.'

'Quite so,' said Mr Potter. 'Bicycle, of course …' His voice tailed off. He was staring at the magic carpet. 'What's that?' he said rather faintly.

'That?' said Mr Majeika cheerily. 'That's my magic –'. He cleared his throat. 'Oh dear, my mistake again. *That's my bicycle.*' And as he said these last words, he pointed a finger at the magic carpet.

There was a funny sort of humming noise, and the carpet rolled itself up and turned into a bicycle.

Mr Majeika leant cheerily against the handlebars and rang the bicycle bell. 'Nice bike, isn't it?' he said, smiling at Mr Potter.

You could have heard a pin drop.

Mr Potter turned rather white. 'I – I don't think I feel very well,' he said at last. 'I – I don't seem to be able to tell the difference between a carpet and a bicycle.'

Mr Majeika smiled even more cheerily. 'Never mind, a very easy mistake to make. And now I think it's time I began to teach our young friends here.'

Mr Potter wiped his forehead with his handkerchief. 'What? Oh – yes – of course,' he muttered faintly, backing to the door. 'Yes, yes, please do begin. Can't tell a bicycle from a carpet …' he mumbled to himself as he left the room.

'Now then,' said Mr Majeika to Class Three, 'to work!'

The Carpet Bicycle. From *Mr Majeika*, by Humphrey Carpenter. Penguin Books Ltd.

THE GHOST TEACHER

The school is closed, the children gone,
But the ghost of a teacher lingers on.
As the daylight fades, as the daytime ends,
As the night draws in and the dark descends,
She stands in the classroom, as clear as glass,
And calls the names of her absent class.

The school is shut, the children grown,
But the ghost of the teacher, all alone,
Puts the date on the board and moves about
(As the night draws on and the stars come out)
Between the desks – a glow in the gloom –
And calls for quiet in the silent room.

The school is a ruin, the children fled,
But the ghost of the teacher, long-time dead,
As the moon comes up and the first owls glide,
Puts on her coat and steps outside.
In the moonlit playground, shadow-free
She stands on duty with a cup of tea.

The school is forgotten – children forget –
But the ghost of a teacher lingers yet.
As the night creeps up to the edge of the day,
She tidies the Plasticine away;
Counts the scissors – a shimmer of glass –
And says, 'Off you go!' to her absent class.

She utters the words that no one hears,
Picks up her bag …
and disappears.

Allan Ahlberg

Activities

A Let's chat

Have you ever been to a magic show or seen one on television? What magic tricks did the magician do? Can you do any magic tricks?

B First impressions

My favourite moment in the story was …

C Seek and search

1 What morning was it in the story?
2 Why was Melanie crying?
3 What flew in the classroom window?
4 What excuse did Mr Majeika give for being late?
5 Name five children in Class Three.

D Quest and query

1 What month of the year do you think it was?
2 How do you know that Mr Potter was annoyed?
3 Would you like Mr Majeika to be your teacher? Explain.
4 If you had Mr Majeika's carpet, to where would you fly?
5 Is 'The Carpet Bicycle' a good title for this story? Why?

E Word watch

When we compare things that are alike in some way, we make an **analogy**, e.g. Melanie is to girl as Pete is to boy.

Choose the correct word in bold to complete the following analogies.

1 Bicycle is to cycling as car is to **washing**, **driving**, **parking**.
2 Monday is to week as January is to **month**, **year**, **summer**.
3 Pupil is to teacher as patient is to **hospital**, **school**, **doctor**.
4 Cry is to sad as laugh is to **joke**, **happy**, **miserable**.
5 First is to last as back is to **end**, **front**, **fourth**.

F Sounds abound

The letters **ch** sometimes make a **/k/** sound, e.g. **Ch**ristmas.

Using squared paper, make a wordsearch with the following words. Use 10 boxes across and 10 boxes down.

school   anchor   ache   chorus   chaos   chemist   echo

G Watch your Ps and Qs

Capital letters are also used for days of the week, months of the year, names of places, and the titles of books and films.

Rewrite this passage using capital letters, full stops, commas and question marks.

it was the first monday in january the pupils were just returning to st barty's primary school after the christmas holidays hamish bigmore was trying to pick a quarrel with thomas and pete pandora green was reading the diary of a wimpy kid 'where is your new teacher' groaned mr potter suddenly in through the window flew mr majeika 'sorry I am late my magic carpet took a wrong turning'

H Flights of fancy

Imagine you are Hamish Bigmore's mother. Write an email to Mr Potter explaining why Hamish is late one day.
Did something magical happen to delay him?   Digital

I Spark starters

1 Find out how your parents/grandparents travelled to school.
2 Find out how different means of transport have developed down through the years.

A Blind Man Catches a Bird

A young man and his blind brother-in-law go out hunting.
The blind man is able to tell many things just by listening
to the sounds of the animals around him. They set traps
to catch birds. The blind man catches a bird that is
beautifully coloured. The other man is very jealous and
swaps the bird with the one he has captured. Will the
blind man find out that his brother-in-law is a thief?

A young man married a woman whose brother was
blind. The young man was eager to get to know his new
brother-in-law and so he asked him if he would like to
go hunting with him.

'I cannot see,' the blind man said. 'But you can help me
see when we are out hunting together. We can go.'

The young man led the blind man off into the bush.
At first they followed a path that he knew and it was easy
for the blind man to tag on behind the other. After a

while, though, they went off into thicker bush, where the
trees grew closely together and there were many places
for the animals to hide. The blind man now held on to
the arm of his sighted brother-in-law and told him many
things about the sounds that they heard around them.
Because he had no sight, he had a great ability to interpret
the noises made by animals in the bush.

'There are warthogs
around,' he would say.
'I can hear their noises
over there.'

Or: 'That bird is preparing
to fly. Listen to the sound of
its wings unfolding.'

To the brother-in-law, these
sounds were meaningless,
and he was most impressed
at the blind man's ability to
understand the bush although
it must have been for him
one great darkness.

175

They walked on for several hours, until they reached a place where they could set their traps. The blind man followed the other's advice, and put his trap in a place where birds might come for water. The other man put his trap a short distance away, taking care to disguise it so

that no bird would know that it was there. He did not bother to disguise the blind man's trap, as it was hot and he was eager to get home to his new wife. The blind man thought that he had disguised his trap, but he did not see that he had failed to do so and any bird could tell that there was a trap there.

They returned to their hunting place the next day. The blind man was excited at the prospect of having caught something, and the young man had to tell him to keep quiet, or he would scare all the animals away. Even before they reached the traps, the blind man was able to tell that they had caught something.

'I can hear birds,' he said. 'There are birds in the traps.'

When he reached his trap, the young man saw that he had caught a small bird. He took it out of the trap and put it in a pouch that he had brought with him. Then the two of them walked towards the blind man's trap.

'There is a bird in it,' he said to the blind man. 'You have caught a bird too.'

As he spoke, he felt himself filling with jealousy. The blind man's bird was marvellously coloured, as if it had flown through a rainbow and been stained by the colours. The feathers from a bird such as that would make a fine present for his new wife, but the blind man had a wife too, and she would also want the feathers.

The young man bent down and took the blind man's bird from the trap. Then, quickly substituting his own bird, he passed it to the blind man and put the coloured bird into his own pouch.

'Here is your bird,' he said to the blind man. 'You may put it in your pouch.'

The blind man reached out for the bird and took it. He felt it for a moment, his fingers passing over the wings and the breast. Then, without saying anything, he put the bird into his pouch and they began the trip home.

On their way home, the two men stopped to rest under a broad tree. As they sat there, they talked about many things. The young man was impressed with the wisdom of the blind man, who knew a great deal, although he could see nothing at all.

'Why do people fight with one another?' he asked the blind man. It was a question which had always troubled him and he wondered if the blind man could give him an answer. The blind man said nothing for a few moments, but it was clear to the young man that he was thinking.

Then the blind man raised his head, and it seemed to the young man as if the unseeing eyes were staring right into his soul. Quietly he gave his answer.

'Men fight because they do to each other what you have just done to me.'

The words shocked the young man and made him ashamed. He tried to think of a response, but none came. Rising to his feet, he fetched his pouch, took out the brightly coloured bird and gave it back to the blind man.

The blind man took the bird, felt over it with his fingers, and smiled.

'Do you have any other questions for me?' he asked.

'Yes,' said the young man. 'How do men become friends after they have fought?'

The blind man smiled again.

'They do what you have just done,' he said. 'That's how they become friends again.'

A Blind Man Catches a Bird. From *Folktales from Africa: The Girl Who Married a Lion*, by Alexander McCall Smith. CanonGate Books Ltd.

Activities

A Let's chat

Did you ever fight or argue with anyone? What was it about? How did you and that person become friends again?

B First impressions

As I read the story I was shocked by …

C Seek and search

1 Why did the young man ask the blind man to go hunting?
2 To where did they go hunting?
3 What were they trying to trap?
4 When did they return to their hunting place?
5 Where did the two men stop to rest?

D Quest and query

1 What does 'he had a great ability to interpret the noises' mean?
2 Why did the young man not disguise the blind man's trap?
3 How did the blind man know there was a bird in his trap?
4 What do you think the wives would do with the feathers?
5 Find the words in the story that mean: (a) keen, (b) frighten, (c) capture, (d) pocket, (e) journey, (f) wide, (g) argued.

E Word watch

Tricky words: **to**, **two**, **too**

Complete the following sentences using the correct words.

1 The _____ men went _____ the bush _____ hunt.
2 The blind man carried a trap and the young man did _____.
3 They caught _____ birds in their traps.
4 The young man had a wife and the blind man did _____.
5 The young man was _____ ashamed _____ admit what he had done.
6 The _____ of them decided _____ head off home.

F Sounds abound

Words are made up of sounds called **syllables**.

Match the syllables and write down the words that they form.

wom	er
dis	pect
broth	an
pros	tance

wis	sponse
wart	dom
re	come
be	hogs

G Watch your Ps and Qs

A **conjunction** joins two sentences, e.g. and/but/because.

Complete the sentences using a conjunction from the box.

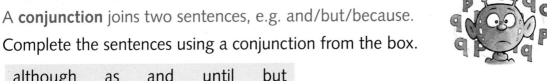

| although | as | and | until | but |

1 The man was a good hunter _____ the blind man was better.

2 The blind man followed his brother-in-law's advice _____ put his trap beside the water.

3 He did not bother to disguise the blind man's trap _____ he was eager to get home.

4 They walked for several hours _____ they reached the traps.

5 The young man was impressed with the wisdom of the blind man _____ he could see nothing at all.

H Flights of fancy

Imagine what the blind man and his brother-in-law say to each other during the story. Write the story in dialogue form. Work in pairs. **Digital**

I Spark starters

1 Find out about warthogs and other African animals.

2 Find out about the ostrich, parrot, flamingo or albatross.

Deserts in Africa

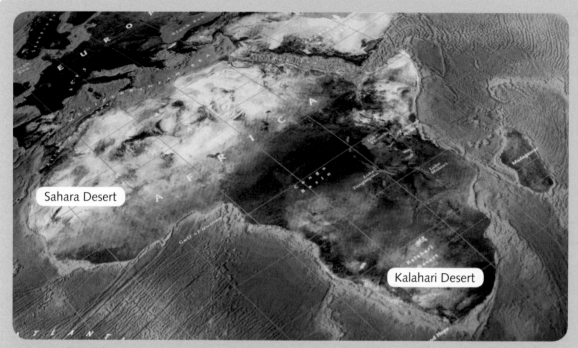

Sahara Desert

Kalahari Desert

There are two large deserts in Africa. The **Sahara Desert** is in the north and the **Kalahari Desert** is in the south. The Sahara is the biggest hot desert in the world. Every year, it grows a bit bigger because of the lack of rain in the surrounding area.

Deserts are hot, sandy places where it hardly ever rains. The Sahara Desert is scorching hot during the day. The temperature can reach up to 50°C. The temperature in the Kalahari Desert can reach about

Sand dunes

Sandstorm

45°C. This is still very hot when you consider that the temperature in Ireland is about 26°C on a very hot day. In both deserts, it is freezing cold at night. Some of the higher sand dunes can even be covered with snow during the winter. Winds blowing across the deserts often stir up sandstorms, which makes life difficult for humans and animals. Very few animals or plants can live in deserts.

However, some plants and animals do survive in the hot, dry desert. The best-known desert plant is the **cactus** (cacti is the plural). The prickly cactus can survive because it has a thick stem that stores water.

Cacti

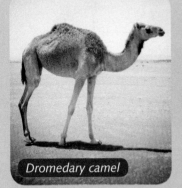
Dromedary camel

The best-known desert animal is the **camel**. In Africa, camels have only one hump. They are called **dromedary** camels. They can travel for days without food or water. They live off the fat they store in their hump.

Other animals that live in the desert include (1) **vultures**, (2) **ostriches**, (3) **meerkats** and (4) **springboks**. There are also (5) **cobras**, (6) **desert foxes** and (7) **jackals**. However, it is mostly small animals, insects and spiders that survive best in the desert. (8) **Scorpions**, (9) **tarantulas** and (10) **locusts** hide underground during the scorching hot days. They come out to hunt at night when it is much cooler.

FACT BOX

Camels with two humps are called bactrian camels. They live in Asia.

Deserts in Africa

A desert oasis, with date palms growing

An **oasis** is a place in the desert where there is water.
Because there is water, people can live there and grow
corn, vegetables and **date palms**.

FACT BOX

The hot sun
in the desert
makes the air
shimmer. This
can make the
sand look like
a lake. This is
called a **mirage**.
Many thirsty
travellers in the
desert have
been fooled by
mirages.

A desert mirage

Most of the people who live in the desert are **nomads**. Nomads are people who travel from place to place to find food and water for themselves and their animals. The nomads who live in the Sahara are **Tuaregs**. They herd camels and goats. They are nicknamed '*The Blue People of the Sahara*' because their cloaks are usually blue. The tents that they live in are made from leather, which they make from animal skins. The tents are held up on strong wooden poles.

Tuareg nomad of the Sahara Desert

Members of the Kalahari Desert Bushmen tribe

The people who live in the Kalahari Desert are called the **Bushmen**. They hunt using bows and arrows. Like all desert people, the Bushmen know the secrets of surviving in the desert. They can suck up water from deep wells or springs below the surface, using hollow sticks. They store water in empty ostrich egg shells. The Bushmen live in huts made of branches covered in straw.

Activities

A **Talk about**

1 Why do you think the Tuaregs and the Bushmen still live in the desert?
2 What would you bring with you in order to survive for one week in the Sahara Desert?
3 What would happen to the nomads if the water in the oases dried up?

B **What have you learned?**

1 Name the two biggest deserts in Africa.
2 What is the temperature like in the deserts at night?
3 Name the prickly plant found in the desert.
4 What type of camel has two humps?
5 Why do tarantulas come out to hunt at night?
6 What causes a mirage?
7 What is an oasis?
8 Why do you think the desert people are nomads?
9 Why are the Tuaregs called 'The Blue People of the Sahara'?
10 How do you think you would survive in the Sahara Desert? Explain your answer.

C **Name the animal**

Name these desert creatures using the words in the box.

| desert fox | vultures | cobra | springbok | jackal | meerkats |

1 _____

2 _____

3 _____

4 _____

5 _____

6 _____

D **True or false**

1 Dromedary camels have two humps. _____

2 A watering hole in the desert is called a mirage. _____

3 The Tuareg people live in the Kalahari Desert. _____

4 Scorpions come out to search for food by day. _____

5 Dromedary camels store water in their hump. _____

E **Complete the sentences**

Rewrite this passage using the correct words from the box.

south	camels	hot	Sahara	oasis	one
dromedary	fat	cold	cactus	goats	nomads

The _____ Desert is in the north of Africa. The Kalahari Desert is in the _____ of Africa. Deserts are very _____ during the day but get very _____ at night. An _____ is a place in the desert where there is water. The camels that live in Africa have _____ hump. They are called _____ camels. They store _____ in their hump. One plant that survives well in the desert is the _____. People who live in the desert are called _____. They travel about the desert with their _____ and _____.

F **Look it up**

Use the Internet to help you answer the following questions.

1 Why are cacti prickly?

2 How does a Namib beetle collect water?

G **Finish the story**

Your jeep has broken down while crossing the Sahara Desert. The battery in your phone is dead. You only have half a flask of water left. You are on your own and a long way from anywhere.

How It All Began

Everyone knows the story of Little Red Riding Hood and The Big Bad Wolf – or at least they think they do. This is the wolf's side of the story. Will you change your mind about The Big Bad Wolf?

My name is Thomas Blake-Burke Wolfe. My friends – when I had any – used to call me Tom.

Though I'm a bit down on my luck at the moment, I come from an old and honoured family. We have lived in the forest for a long, long time.

Once the name Wolfe used to mean a lot around here.

Not since I came along! I blame it all on the Three Little Pigs and their lies. They started it. Then everyone jumped on the band-wagon.

Now I'm known everywhere as The Big Bad Wolf. People hiss and boo when I pass. *They're* the ones invited to tea at the castle and lunch with the Lord Mayor.

What happened wasn't my fault. I'm a very nice wolf really. But lately everything that happens in these parts is blamed on me.

I'm the innocent victim of circumstances. That's why I want to set the record straight.

I well remember the first spot of bother I had with those three porkers. It happened shortly after they moved into the forest. They were wild right from the start, always causing trouble.

I had gone over to Red Riding Hood's cottage deep in the forest. I had heard her grandmother wasn't at all well and I thought I would take her out to lunch. Cheer her up a bit.

I'm that kind of bloke.

But as soon as I opened the front door – she keeps the key under the flower-pot on the window-sill – she started to scream at the top of her voice.

'Help! Help! It's The Big Bad Wolf!'

It was the first time anyone had ever called me that.
I was gobsmacked.

Try as I might, I could not stop her squealing like a
Sioux Indian. In the end I thought I'd try a bit of flattery.

'My, what big eyes you have, Granny,' I cooed.

That went down like a lead balloon.

'I know what you're after,' she managed to get out,
in between the screams. Her high-pitched voice left my
ears ringing.

'I just wanted to have you for lunch, dear lady,' I said
in a fawning voice.

That really hit the jackpot.

'Help! Help! Help! The Big Bad Wolf is going to gobble
me up,' she shrieked.

I couldn't understand where I had gone wrong? Too late it hit me.

I had said: 'to have you *for* lunch.'

I had meant to say: 'to have you *out* for lunch.'

Just then, something else hit me. Her big, heavy, frying pan.

Luckily I caught it. Otherwise it would have sliced my head off.

I grabbed it and used it to fend off all the other things she was throwing at me, in between trying to duck out through the front door.

I was half in and half out, dodging cups, saucers, plates and saucepans when who should come along, skipping and singing, but the Three Little Pigs.

Before I could explain what was happening, they dashed off to the woodcutter, who was working nearby, and told him that I was killing Little Red Riding Hood's grandmother.

Now I ask you …

Two minutes later, this huge woodcutter turned up at full gallop, waving an axe as big as himself.

He was shouting such vile abuse that I had to shut my ears. I have never heard language like it since or before.

No way could I explain myself. I had to run for my life, fast as my legs could carry me, with this raging madman after me.

I wasn't the better of it for weeks.

Of course I told everyone the true story of what had happened.

Do you think anyone believed me?

And afterwards, that little biddy, Red Riding Hood, went around telling anyone who hadn't heard the story that I had attacked her poor old defenceless granny, and that only for the Three Little Pigs I would have gobbled her up, false teeth and all.

How nasty can you get?

The True Story of the Three Little Pigs and the Big Bad Wolf, by Liam Farrell, 2001.
Mercier Press Ltd Cork.

193

The Dinosaur's Dinner

Once a mighty dinosaur
Came to dine with me,
He gobbled up the curtains
And swallowed our settee.

He didn't seem to fancy
Onion soup with crusty bread,
He much preferred the flavour
Of our furniture instead.

He ate up all our dining chairs
And carpets from the floor
He polished off the table, then
He looked around for more.

The television disappeared
In one almighty gulp,
Wardrobes, beds and bathroom
He crunched into a pulp.

He really loved the greenhouse
He liked the garden shed,
He started on the chimney-pots
But then my mother said:

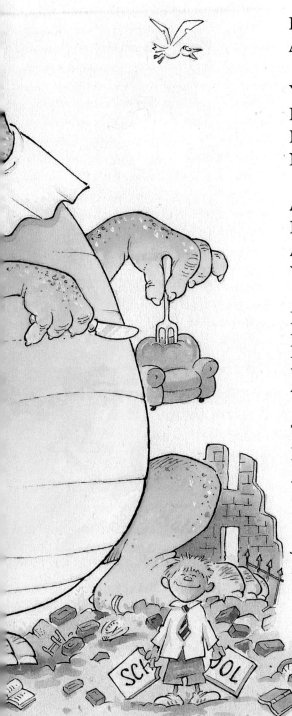

'Your friends are always welcome
To drop in for a bite,
But really this one seems to have
A giant appetite.

You'd better take him somewhere else,
I'm sure I don't know where,
I only know this friend of yours
Needs more than we can spare!'

And suddenly I realised
I knew the very place,
And when I showed him where it was
You should have seen his face –

I don't think I've seen anyone
Enjoy a dinner more,
I watched him wander on his way,
A happy dinosaur!

The council did rebuild our school,
But that of course took time …
And all because a dinosaur
Came home with me to dine!

June Crebbin
(From *The Crocodile is Coming*, 2005)

Activities

A Let's chat

Think of a time when you and your friend
saw a situation differently. What happened?
How did you resolve your difference of opinion?

B First impressions

This story is similar to …

C Seek and search

1 What is the wolf's name?
2 Who does he blame for telling lies?
3 What nickname does he use for the Three Little Pigs?
4 What did Red Riding Hood's grandmother first scream?
5 Who came along? What did they do?

D Quest and query

1 Where did Thomas get the key to the cottage door?
2 How do we know that the Three Little Pigs were happy?
3 What, besides the frying pan, did the grandmother throw?
4 How do we know that the woodcutter was angry?
5 Is it important to listen to all sides of a story? Why?

E Word watch

Match the following phrases with their meaning.

Word

1 jump on the bandwagon	(a) succeed
2 hit the jackpot	(b) follow the popular thing
3 set the record straight	(c) speechless
4 go down like a lead balloon	(d) having a bad time
5 down on my luck	(e) tell the true facts
6 gobsmacked	(f) fail completely

F Sounds abound

Unscramble these syllables to make real words from the story.

1 cent-inn-o _____

2 cum-cir-stance _____

3 vi-ted-in _____

4 y-ter-flat _____

5 ter-wards-af _____

6 less-fence-de _____

7 ter-cut-wood _____

8 ed-smack-gob _____

9 er-wise-oth _____

10 y-luck-il _____

G Watch your Ps and Qs

To make the plural form of a word that ends in **f/fe**, change the **f/fe** to **v** and add **es**, e.g. wol**f**/wol**ves**, kni**fe**/kni**ves**.

1 Write the plural of the following words.

(a) wolf _____

(b) wife _____

(c) scarf _____

(d) calf _____

(e) leaf _____

(f) half _____

2 Write the singular of the following words.

(a) leaves _____

(b) shelves _____

(c) thieves _____

(d) lives _____

(e) loaves _____

(f) elves _____

H Flights of fancy

Write a book report about your favourite fairy tale. Include the name of the fairy tale, the setting, the main characters, the minor characters, a conflict/problem, what they do to overcome it, and how does it end?   Digital

I Spark starters

1 Find out about Sioux Indians or another Native American tribe. Where/how do they live? What language do they speak? What do they hunt?

2 Find out about some forests throughout the world.

Wanted!
The Hundred-Mile-An-Hour Dog

Streaker, the fastest dog in the world, is in trouble again. She has stolen a chicken. Trevor, her owner, must face a very angry man. Then he must come home to face his parents. How will he get out of this tricky situation? What will Streaker get up to next to cause more trouble for poor Trevor?

So, there I was, lying on my front, in a rain puddle, in the middle of the High Street, with a dog standing on my back. Streaker had a roast chicken jammed in her jaws and looked immensely pleased with herself. I closed my eyes and groaned. Could this get any worse? In short – yes.

'Where did you get that chicken from?' I hissed.

She couldn't answer of course. Her mouth was full.
Besides, she didn't need to, because at that moment I saw
the answer hurtling towards me – a very big man with a
body built like a monster truck.

Streaker took one look at the approaching human
juggernaut and *fwooooosh*! She'd vanished, complete with
her packed lunch. She couldn't have run faster if she'd
been shot from a cannon.

'Streaker!' I yelled.

Monster-truck man skidded to a halt right next to me.
He was bright red, roaring and blowing as if all his
exhaust pipes had fallen off. 'Was that your dog?' he
thundered. Gulp! Time for an instant decision. Should I
tell the truth or should I just pretend for a bit? I glanced at
the man's bulging muscles. I looked at his swollen, angry
face. I decided to pretend, otherwise I might die on the
spot, and I hadn't made my funeral arrangements.

'That dog? No,' I squeaked.

'You called her. How do you know her name if she's not
your dog?'

'Um – seen her before. She gets everywhere. I don't know who she belongs to, but I heard someone call her name once and I remembered it. She mugged me. She jumped me from behind and shoved me in a puddle. I'm soaking. Mum'll be mad.'

The man stared after the vanishing cloud of dust. 'Pesky dog stole my roast chicken. I'd only just bought it. Stole it right out of my bag. That was my lunch.'

'Dogs,' I grunted. 'What can you do? Nothing but bother.'

The man searched my face. 'You sure that dog isn't yours?'

'If I had a dog like that, I'd be in serious trouble,' I pointed out to him, quite pleased with myself really because this wasn't pretending at all. It was only too true.

The man's shoulders slumped forward as he calmed down, and he scratched his head. 'Straight out of my bag, a whole roast chicken – gone. Now what am I going to do?'

'Better get another one,' I suggested.

The man raised his eyebrows and nodded. 'Suppose I better had.' He growled, took a swipe at nothing with one big boot, then trudged back up the street. 'If you see that dog again, give it a big kick from me,' he grunted by way of saying goodbye.

Give Streaker a big kick? No way! Streaker was the best dog in the whole world! It was just that she was a bit unpredictable. And uncontrollable. And a general nuisance. And a criminal and a lot more besides. Even so, you couldn't help loving her – at least I couldn't. Streaker is the cleverest dog I know, and I know, well, at least two dogs. She is probably the cleverest dog in Doggy Land.

When I got home Streaker was already there, sitting on the front step with a cheerful grin on her face, surrounded by bits of chicken carcass. Mum stuck her head out of the front window and made a stern announcement.

'She brought a roast chicken home, Trevor. Has she been stealing again?'

'She doesn't know it's stealing, Mum,' I explained.
'She's a dog.'

'I wouldn't let her come in – not with a roast chicken.
I made her sit outside. What are you going to do with her?'

Don't you love it when parents are faced with a problem
and they ask you: what are YOU going to do about it?
They never ask themselves, do they? If you want my
opinion, parents should take on a lot more responsibility.

'Perhaps it's a phase she's going through,' I suggested.
'She never used to steal food. It only started recently.
I blame it on Charlie Smugg's Alsatians.'

Charlie Smugg is the son of our local policeman,
Sergeant Smugg. They have three Alsatians in their
house. Three! They're always chasing Streaker and they'd
been having a real go at her lately, encouraged by Charlie,
of course. 'Look, there's breakfast!' he'd shout.
'Go, Hounds of Death!' You've probably gathered that
Charlie and his dad are not exactly my best friends.

Anyhow, Charlie's Alsatians got Streaker trapped behind the public loos in the park a few weeks ago. They'd already chased her way across the park and I was miles behind. There was nothing I could do to help her. I heard a lot of growling and squeaks. I was frantic. Then the Alsatians came charging back out and suddenly there was Streaker up on the roof of all places.

From *Wanted! The Hundred-Mile-An-Hour Dog*, by Jeremy Strong. Puffin Books.

Activities

A Let's chat

What excuse would you make up if your dog:
(a) stole sausages from the shop; (b) tore your mum's dress;
(c) ate your homework; (d) stole a cake from your neighbour?

B First impressions

The funniest thing about this story was …

C Seek and search

1 Name the dog in the story.
2 Who was chasing her? Why?
3 What did Trevor suggest that the man do?
4 Who is Charlie Smugg? Is he a friend of Trevor's?
5 Where did Streaker go when the Alsatians chased her?

D Quest and query

1 Why did Trevor not tell the man that he owned Streaker?
2 How do you know Streaker had stolen something before?
3 Why do you think Streaker had a cheerful grin?
4 Choose two words/phrases used to describe the man.
5 Choose two words/phrases used to describe Streaker.

E Word watch

Solve the following riddles.

1 What is both the name of an ogre and means huge?
   (a) enormous, (b) monster, (c) massive, (d) fiend

2 What has four legs and barks?
   (a) a cat, (b) a rabbit, (c) a dog, (d) a tree

3 What can describe part of the mouth or part of a building?
   (a) teeth, (b) floor, (c) roof, (d) tongue

4 What rhymes with punch and is a midday meal?
   (a) dinner, (b) breakfast, (c) lunch, (d) supper

Word

F Sounds abound

Unscramble the following sentences that contain **str** words.

1 world. **Str**eaker fastest dog the the in was
2 High **Str**eet. ran up **Str**eaker
3 chicken took She a a **str**aight of out bag. man's
4 **str**ong as man as an ox. The was
5 Trevor **str**eet. **str**olled down the
6 **Str**eaker **str**eam. **str**etched out the beside

G Watch your Ps and Qs

A **contraction** is used in place of two words. An **apostrophe** is used to show where the letters are missing, e.g. let's = let us; I'm = I am; it's = it is.

Rewrite the following sentences using contractions instead of the underlined words.

1 Streaker <u>could not</u> answer.
2 Are you sure that dog <u>is not</u> yours?
3 She <u>does not</u> know <u>it is</u> stealing.
4 I <u>would not</u> let her come in.
5 Perhaps <u>it is</u> a phase <u>she is</u> going through.
6 '<u>She is</u> only a dog you know,' I said.

H Flights of fancy

Design an advertisement to find a dog trainer for Streaker. Describe her and what you would like her to be able to do.

Digital

I Spark starters

Find out about (a) companion dogs, (b) guard dogs, (c) hunting dogs, (d) herding dogs, (e) working dogs or (f) dogs for helping the blind.

Superfast Animals

Superfast Animals on Land

Many wild animals face a daily struggle to survive. Their world is full of danger. As a result, many animals have learned to run fast to get away from danger. The best hunters in the world must also be very fast, if they are to catch the food that they need in order to survive.

A cheetah

The world's fastest land animal is the **cheetah**. This beautiful, spotted cat is very fast. Animals such as **gazelles** are at high risk of attack from cheetahs out on the grassy **plains** of Africa.

A gazelle

FACT BOX

The cheetah's excellent eyesight is very helpful when hunting. It is the only member of the cat family, other than the domestic cat, that purrs. It might not be a good idea to keep one as a pet though!

The cheetah is not as big as a lion or a tiger. It is thin and sleek. It will sit in long grass, waiting for other animals to pass close by. Its lovely black spots help it to hide in the grass. If an animal, such as a gazelle, gets close enough, the cheetah will break into a superfast run. It can run at up to 120 kilometres per hour. That is the highest speed limit for cars in Ireland! The cheetah can keep up this speed for a few hundred metres, but then it has to slow down. It will usually catch its prey.

Superfast Animals in the Air

The **peregrine falcon** is the fastest animal in the sky, when it is swooping for prey. Some peregrine falcons live in Ireland. They were once quite rare but there are more in the world nowadays. The peregrine falcon has really good eyesight and can see even tiny things from very far away.

It flies very high into the sky. Once it is high enough, it can glide and soar through the air, looking down below. If it sees a bird, such as a pigeon, flapping along below, it will get ready to attack. This attack is fast and deadly.

Peregrine falcon in flight

The peregrine falcon folds its wings back so that they become quite small. It leans forward into a sharp dive. It becomes like a living dart. A diving falcon can reach speeds of up to 300 kilometres per hour, making it the fastest animal alive.

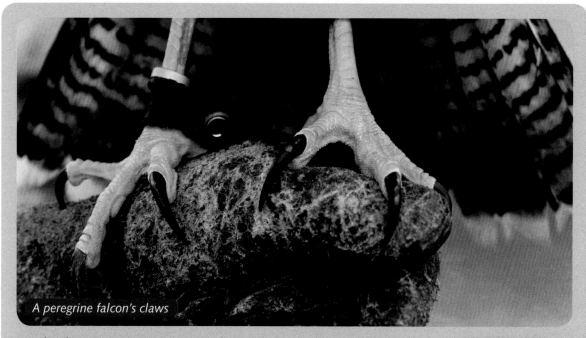
A peregrine falcon's claws

At the last moment, it spreads out its wings to stop the dive. It strikes its prey with its claws closed like fists for a killer punch. The other bird is killed in an instant. It is grabbed in mid-air and carried away in the falcon's sharp claws.

Peregrine falcons often hunt starlings, pigeons, ducks and doves. They have to do a lot of hunting when they have young chicks to look after. A pair of falcons will make their nest high up on a cliff or even on top of a tall building. They might have up to four chicks to feed. Not only can they fly very fast, they can also travel very far.

FACT BOX

Hunting birds like the falcon are called birds of prey.

FACT BOX

Peregrine falcons can fly more than 25,000 kilometres in a year. That is more than half way around the world!

A peregrine falcon chick in a nest

Superfast Animals in the Seas and Oceans

The **Indo-Pacific sailfish** lives in the Pacific Ocean. It is the fastest creature in the sea and ocean. Very little is known about it because it spends a lot of time travelling long distances far out at sea. It hunts fish such as mackerel or tuna, which live together in large groups called **schools** or **shoals**.

Indo-Pacific sailfish

The Indo-Pacific sailfish has a very big tail. It will shoot through a school of fish at nearly 120 kilometres per hour. It eats the smaller fish in the blink of an eye. Sometimes, groups of Indo-Pacific sailfish will work together as a team. They will swim around a school of smaller fish, making them swim close together. They then zip and dart through the school until all have had enough to eat.

A school of mackerel fish

FACT BOX

Indo-Pacific sailfish are not usually eaten by humans (if they are caught). This is because their meat is very tough.

As you can see, out in the wild, extra speed can mean the difference between life and death.

Activities

A Talk about

1 Talk about some very fast animals that you know about.
2 Talk about some sea creatures that are mammals.
3 Talk about a trip you made to the cat section of a zoo.
4 How might peregrine falcons be a menace to farmers?

B What have you learned?

1 What is the fastest land animal in the world?
2 How fast can it travel?
3 What helps a cheetah to hide in the long grass?
4 Name an animal that cheetahs like to hunt.
5 What is the fastest creature in the sky?
6 How do you think a peregrine falcon's claws help it when hunting?
7 What is the fastest creature in the seas and oceans?
8 What type of fish does the Indo-Pacific sailfish hunt?
9 Give one reason why it is a good idea for fish to live in schools.
10 Give one reason why it might be a bad idea for fish to live in schools.

C True or false

1 The peregrine falcon lives in Ireland. _____
2 The Indo-Pacific sailfish is the fastest animal in the world. _____
3 A cheetah is bigger than a lion. _____
4 A peregrine falcon can travel as fast as 500 kilometres per hour. _____
5 You can find Indo-Pacific sailfish in the waters around Ireland. _____
6 Mackerel live in large groups called schools. _____
7 A peregrine falcon has blunt claws. _____
8 The Indo-Pacific sailfish has a small tail. _____

D Mixed-up sentences

Sort out the following mixed-up sentences.
1 sleek. thin The is cheetah and
2 peregrine falcon the high flies in The sky.
3 hunt schools smaller fish. Indo-Pacific sailfish of

E Complete the sentences

Rewrite this passage using the correct words from the box.

hunt	tail	speed	dart	school	animals
sailfish	falcon	groups	food	together	

The Indo-Pacific _____ is able to speed through the water.

It has a very big _____. It likes to hunt in _____. It will swim

around a _____ of smaller fish and make them swim close

_____ in a group. Then the Indo-Pacific sailfish will _____

and zip through them, eating one small fish after another.

A cheetah will _____ while hiding in long grass.

The peregrine _____ hunts while flying high in the sky.

All of these _____ use _____ to catch their _____.

F Look it up

Use the Internet to help you find the following information.
1 How are falcons in Ireland affected by farmers?
2 Find out about another bird of prey that lives in Ireland.
3 Find some details about barracudas, manta rays, blue marlins and
   other strange fish of the sea.

G Finish the story

It was a hot, sunny day. The cheetah was feeling hungry.

Spy Dog

Lara is a very intelligent dog. Lara, or GM451 as she is also known, is in Phase One of spy school. She is beginning to enjoy herself after a successful mountain rescue. Professor Cortex has to choose one dog to go forward to Phase Two. What will happen when a burglar attempts to steal the professor's top dog and all the vital information he has stored on his computer hard drive?

The successful mountain rescue had changed Lara's attitude to spy school. *If I'm chosen for Phase Two, I'll get a life of excitement, action and adventure. Think of all the good I could do, all the criminals I could put behind bars and all the fun I could have.* Lara decided to focus her efforts on showing her true talents.

Her first opportunity to shine came that very night. The professor locked up and switched off the light. The dogs settled down for the night. Lara lay on her bed and thought about spy school. She knew the professor and his team would choose just one dog to go forward to the next level of training. She'd heard them talking about it and knew that she was in second place. *I just hope I haven't left it too late.* She nodded off, dreaming of chasing baddies.

Lara woke with a start and glanced at the clock. She hadn't quite mastered telling the time yet, but the big hand was on the twelve and the little hand was on the two. She knew it was very late. She came to her senses and pricked up her ears. The other dogs snored on. One of the farm dogs was particularly noisy, whining and twitching in his sleep, obviously rounding up sheep. *There's the noise again, very faint but getting louder. It sounds like footsteps tiptoeing outside.* Lara cocked her head to listen.

Suddenly there was a loud crash and a brick came through the window, glass showering the floor. The dogs all awoke and started yapping. *Calm down, you lot*, barked Lara, trying to concentrate on what was going on. A gloved hand appeared through the broken window and undid the catch. The window swung open and a shadowy figure climbed in. The yapping frenzy increased.

Lara stayed calm. *The professor and his team have some very valuable equipment and I bet the data on his computer is worth a fortune.*

The shadow man moved swiftly around the lab, his boots crunching on the glass. He shone his torch into some of the cages. 'Silence, dogs,' he cursed. 'I'm stealing to order. I only need one of you. In fact, I only need the top dog.' He stepped between the cages until he found the one he was looking for.

He fumbled with a bunch of keys and unlocked
PX772's cage, before clipping a lead on to his collar and
tying the other end to a chair. PX772
sat obediently while the caged dogs
barked furiously. As the shadow man
moved towards the computer, Lara
decided she must take action. *I can't just
sit by and let this burglar get away with the
professor's hard work, can I?*

She jumped on to her bed and pulled
the pillow aside. There was the key to
her cage. (She always kept a spare in
case of emergencies. *You just never know,*

she'd thought as she took it from the
professor's pocket.)

Lara picked up the key in her
mouth and inserted it in the keyhole.
She twisted her head and unlocked the
cage door, pushing it open with
her nose.

The burglar obviously knew what he was after. He didn't want the whole computer, just the information on the hard drive. He unscrewed the computer and got what he had come for. *He's got the top-scoring dog and all the professor's data*, thought Lara. *I can't let him get away with it.*

'Come on, mutt, let's get out of here,' he said to PX772, untying him from the chair.

Not if I can help it, thought Lara. She leapt out of the shadows and sank her teeth into the man's ankle. The burglar cursed and kicked out, dropping the drive. Lara picked the drive up and scurried back into her cage, hiding it under her pillow. The man flashed his torch in her direction. 'Give me that hard drive, mutt,' he said. 'It's very valuable.'

Come and get it then, she thought, tempting him into
her cage.

The man was wary. He wasn't sure whether Lara would
bite him again, so he edged carefully into the cage, feeling
his way in the dark. 'Nice puppy,' he soothed, trying to
keep himself and the dog calm. 'Give me the disk like a
nice pup.'

Lara took her chance and trotted out, leaving him to
scrabble under the pillow. By the time he'd pocketed the
drive, Lara had carefully closed the cage door and locked
it, then swallowed the key.

The burglar watched as she gulped the key down.
He was beside himself with rage. 'What … How …?' he
blustered. 'Let me out, you stupid mutt!' he yelled …

Hang on, thought Lara. *I'm out here and you're locked in
the cage, so who's the stupid one?*

Lara barked for the other animals to be quiet. *Everyone, please, the excitement's over. This silly man was trying to rob the professor and steal PX772. Let's get some sleep, and we'll sort this mess out in the morning.*

The noise subsided and the dogs eventually went back to sleep. All was quiet, except for the noise Lara made as she swept up the mess.

The professor was in bright and early. He lived for his work and was annoyed that sleep had to get in the way. He placed his thumb on the security pad and the door slid open. His eyes widened as he saw Lara helping herself to some cornflakes while the other dogs waited obediently for their breakfast. A man dressed in black was locked in Lara's cage. The professor looked at the man, who just shrugged.

To Lara's amazement, the professor went over to the cage and unlocked it, helping the shadow man out. 'Good morning, Agent B,' the professor greeted him. 'Let me make you a coffee and you can tell me all about Operation Break-in.'

Now Lara was excited. This was the first time she'd seen how crafty real agents could be. The professor had set up the whole burglary scene, just to test the reactions of the dogs.

Agent B described the entire operation. He explained how PX772 had been so pathetic, allowing himself to be unlocked and then tied up. He described how ten dogs yapped in fury and how one black-and-white puppy took charge. The professor listened, open-mouthed, as he heard how Lara had escaped from her cage, rescued the disk and trapped Agent B. 'And where's the key she used?' asked the astonished professor.

Agent B coughed. 'Erm … well, you should get it back in a day or two, sir,' he said, opening his mouth and dropping in an imaginary key.

Professor Cortex raised his bushy eyebrows in amazement. He walked over to Lara and shook her warmly by the paw.

'GM451,' he said, 'our search is over. I would be delighted if you will do me the honour of joining me in Phase Two of the spy-dog programme. You, young lady, are our top dog.'

Lara nodded her acceptance. *Prof*, she thought, *if you make it as exciting as last night, I'd be delighted.*

From *Spy Dog*, by Andrew Cope. Puffin Books.

The Guide Dog's Story

'Young Catherine has lost her sight,
and now her world is dark as night.

I am well trained. I am her guide.
Together we walk side by side.

Young Catherine has lost her sight.
Each sunny day is black as night.

I let her know where danger lies.
I am the blind girl's seeing eyes.'

Wes Magee

Activities

A Let's chat

Would you like to go to Spy School? Why? What would you like to learn there? What equipment would you need to become a spy? What do you know about spying?

B First impressions

I liked/disliked this story because …

C Seek and search

1 Name the main dog in the story.
2 What woke all of the dogs?
3 What two things did the burglar want to steal?
4 What was the number of the top dog?
5 Who had set up Operation Break-in?

D Quest and query

1 Why did Lara want to be chosen for Phase Two?
2 How many dogs were in Spy School?
3 Why do you think the burglar was wearing gloves?
4 How did Lara come to have a spare key?
5 Do you think Operation Break-in was successful? Explain.

E Word watch

A **prefix** is a group of letters at the beginning of a word that usually changes its meaning, e.g. able/unable, play/replay.

| un | re | de | be |

Rewrite the following sentences using the correct prefix.

1 Lara was ___lighted to be in Spy School.

2 A gloved hand ___did the catch on the window.

3 Lara ___acted immediately and ___locked her cage.

4 Lara watched him ___tying PX772 from ___neath the chair.

Word

222

F Sounds abound

If you hear the sound **shun** in a word, it is usually spelt **tion**.
Crack the code for these words which end in **tion**.

a	c	d	e	f	i	m	n	o	p	r	t
1	2	3	4	5	6	7	8	9	10	11	12

(a) 6, 8, 5, 9, 11, 7, 1, 12, 6, 9, 8. _____

(b) 3, 6, 11, 4, 2, 12, 6, 9, 8. _____

(c) 11, 4, 1, 2, 12, 6, 9, 8. _____

(d) 9, 10, 4, 11, 1, 12, 6, 9, 8. _____

(e) 1, 12, 12, 4, 8, 12, 6, 9, 8. _____

G Watch your Ps and Qs

Verbs (action words) change depending on when the action happened, e.g. The professor <u>knows</u> the dogs (present tense). The professor <u>knew</u> the dogs (past tense).

Match the present tense verbs to their past tense form.

hear	woke
bring	stole
steal	came
wake	brought
come	heard

think	did
see	was
is	saw
do	found
find	thought

H Flights of fancy

You are going undercover on a mission. Decide what/where your mission will be. Who/what will you bring with you?   Digital

I Spark starters

Send a message to another spy. Write it in lemon juice. Let it dry. Heat the paper over a light bulb to read the message.

The Giant's Wife

Fionn McCool, a famous Irish giant, lived with his wife Una in County Tyrone. Across the sea in Scotland, another giant heard the people boasting about how big and strong Fionn was. The Scottish giant decided to visit Ireland to pay Fionn a visit. Would Una be able to save her husband or would there be all-out war between the two giants?

Long ago there was a giant called Fionn McCool, and Fionn McCool lived with his wife, Una, in a big house in the County Tyrone. Across the sea in Scotland there lived another giant, and he lived in a cave on the windy hillside and not in a house at all.

Now, Fionn McCool was a big giant. He was as tall as a ten-storey house and as wide as the side of a lorry. His head was the size of a cinema screen and his little toe was as big as a doorstep. And he could run a hundred miles without getting puffed. Everyone in the neighbourhood used to boast about how big he was, so his fame soon spread through the four provinces of Ireland. And pretty soon it spread across the sea to Scotland as well.

One morning, Una found Fionn sitting at the kitchen table in front of his tub of porridge. He always had porridge for breakfast because there weren't any cornflakes in those days. Even if there had been, it would have taken twenty boxes to fill Fionn.

He wasn't eating breakfast. He was just sitting there gloomily, chewing his thumbs. Una was very surprised.

'What's the matter with you?' she said. 'Is the porridge lumpy?'

'No, it's grand,' said Fionn. 'But I've just had some news that's put me right off it.'

'What's that?' said Una.

Fionn asked her if she'd ever heard of the Scottish Giant.

'Of course I have,' said Una. 'I know all about him. He's a big, huge, fierce giant, even bigger than you are. And he's got wild, shaggy red hair and great, jagged, broken teeth and a big, knotted ash stick that's longer than a double-decker bus.'

'But what's he got to do with your breakfast?' she asked.

'He's coming to bash me up,' wailed Fionn. 'He says he's fed up of hearing about me.'

You see, the Scottish Giant had heard the people of Tyrone boasting about how big and strong Fionn was. So he'd decided to pay him a visit and see for himself.

'Well, that'll teach you not to go boasting about how big you are,' said Una.

'I don't,' said Fionn. 'Well, maybe I do a bit. But what am I going to do now?' he said. 'He'll be halfway here already.'

'Hold your whisht and have your breakfast,' said she. 'I'll think of something.'

And she did.

She left Fionn to light the fire and heat the oven, and off she went to the neighbour's house to borrow a griddle.

A griddle is a round, flat pan made of iron. People used them to bake bread over the fire.

Now, when Una had borrowed the biggest griddle she could find, she rushed back home to bake some bread. But when her loaf was shaped she pulled it in half and hid the griddle inside the dough. Then she baked it in the oven. So when it came out it had the hardest centre of any loaf ever made.

Then she made several other loaves as well, delicious, ordinary loaves that were crusty outside and soft within.

And then she sat down by the fire to do some sewing.

When she was finished, she held up a giant nightdress and a baby's cap that she'd made out of a tablecloth. Then she dressed Fionn up as a baby and tucked him up in a wicker basket by the fire.

Now Fionn had no idea what she was up to. But he did what she told him and he kept his mouth shut. As soon as he was in the basket, there was a knock on the door. And there was the Scottish Giant with his big stick.

Una smiled at him and she rocked the basket with her toe.

'Yes?' she said, 'were you looking for someone?'

And he told her he was looking for Fionn McCool.

'I'm afraid he's out at the moment,' said Una. 'He's just gone to knock down the town at the end of the valley.'

The Giant was impressed.

'Maybe you'd like to sit down and wait?' said Una.
'He'll only be ten minutes. Will you have a cup of tea in
your hand?'

The Scottish Giant said he'd be delighted. But he was
a little worried because *he* didn't think he could flatten
a whole town in ten minutes. And it seemed that Fionn
could. So maybe it wasn't going to be that easy to bash
him up after all.

Una got up to put the kettle on the fire. Then she shook
her head sadly.

'Would you look at that,' she said. 'The wind's in the
west again. Now if only Fionn were here he'd turn the
house around. As it is, the fire will smoke and we'll have
smoky tea.'

She sighed and she looked at the Scottish Giant.
And what could he do but offer to help?

So up he got and off he went outside. And he shoved
and he heaved and he hauled and he pushed until the
house was turned right round.

By this time he was really worried. It was awfully hard
turning that house. And Una had behaved as if Fionn did
it easily. Meanwhile Fionn was shivering in his basket.
You see, he'd never turned the house round in his life.
He wouldn't have been strong enough.

As soon as the giant sat down again, Una gave him his tea.

'Here's a new-made loaf to go with it,' she said. And she
handed him the loaf with the griddle in it.

He took a big bite. Then his tooth hit the griddle with
an awful crack and he let a roar out of him that shook the
house from attic to cellar.

'What's the matter?' said Una.

'Glory be to God, ma'am,' said the Scottish Giant, 'that bread's like iron.'

'Nonsense,' said Una. 'I only made it this morning. Sure the baby could eat that and come to no harm.'

She turned away and crossed to the basket by the fire. Then she picked up one of the ordinary loaves and handed it to Fionn. And Fionn ate the loaf in two bites.

The Scottish Giant couldn't believe his eyes. He rushed over to the basket and then jumped back in alarm.

'That's a grand big baby, ma'am,' he said nervously. 'What age is he?'

Una shook her head.

'Oh it's nice of you to say so,' she said, 'but he's not big at all for six months. Sure, his Daddy's ashamed of the size he is.'

'And is that a bit of the Daddy's bread he's after chewing?' said the Giant.

'It is,' said Una. 'He's got a grand set of teeth in his head, thank God. Fionn had all his teeth at two weeks, of course, but this lad's not doing badly. Would you like to feel them?' And she took his hand and guided it into Fionn's mouth.

Well Fionn mightn't have been as clever as his wife but he wasn't a fool altogether. He knew what to do when he felt the Scottish Giant's hand between his teeth. He bit him. He bit him as hard and as long as he could. And he didn't stop till the Giant was howling for mercy.

Una let on to be horrified.

'Oh, God forgive you, you bold child,' she said. 'Is it biting the nice gentleman and he only trying to be friendly? Just wait till your Daddy gets home.'

But if that was the baby, the Scottish Giant wasn't waiting to see the Daddy. He was out of the house and away down the road before Una had finished speaking. And he didn't stop running till he was back in his own cave on the windy hillside in the north of Scotland.

The Giant's Wife, by Felicity Hayes McCoy.

Activities

A Let's chat

Do you think it is a good idea to boast? Why? How would your friends feel if you are always boasting?

B First impressions

My favourite character in the story is … because …

C Seek and search

1 Where did Fionn and his wife, Una, live?
2 What news had Fionn just heard?
3 Where did Una get the griddle pan?
4 What did Una hide in the dough?
5 Where did Una say that Fionn was that day?
6 How old did Una say the baby was?

D Quest and query

1 Why did Fionn always have porridge for breakfast?
2 How do we know that Una was a 'bright' woman?
3 Why did Una put the griddle inside the dough?
4 Why did the Scottish Giant try to turn the house around?
5 Did the Scottish Giant believe that Fionn was a baby? Explain.
6 Which was the braver of the two giants? Explain.

E Word watch

Write the following sentences removing the incorrect words, e.g. The man jumped over under the wall.

1 Fionn was as tall wide as a ten-storey house.
2 Una saw Fionn sitting walking gloomily at the table.
3 Una borrowed the biggest griddle she could bake find.
4 She tucked Fionn up in a tablecloth wicker basket.
5 The giant was delighted worried to have a cup of tea.
6 The giant did not begin stop running till he was back in his cave.

Word

F Sounds abound

From the story, find 10 words containing 2, 3 or 4 syllables (multisyllabic words) in this word snake.

o p i m p r e s s e d c g b o a s t i n g d s i n f o r m a t i o n f
g o r d i n a r y w t n e r v o u s l p o f r i e n d l y f g s h i v e r i n g b g
n e i g h b o u r h o o d h m g e n t l e m a n s w a l t o g e t h e r

G Watch your Ps and Qs

A **simile** is a comparison of two unlike things using the word **as**, e.g. Fionn was **as** tall as a ten-storey house.

Complete the following similes using the correct words.

1 As round as a _____. triangle, circle, square, rectangle

2 As sly as a _____. fox, dog, bear, chicken

3 As old as the _____. building, school, man, hills

4 As hungry as a _____. wolf, lamb, hen, sheep

5 As mad as the March _____. hare, rabbit, badger, squirrel

H Flights of fancy

1 Write a short summary of how Una tricked the Scottish Giant. `Digital`

2 Write a list of things you might find in the Scottish Giant's cave.

I Spark starters

1 Find out about the Giant's Causeway.

2 Read the story 'The Tortoise and the Hare' from Aesop's Fables. Who was always boasting in this story? What is the moral of the story?

Famous Irish Landmarks

The Giant's Causeway

The **Giant's Causeway** is in County Antrim in Northern Ireland. Every year, thousands of visitors come to see the strange and fascinating columns of rock that jut out into the sea. About 40,000 rocks make up the Giant's Causeway. They are mainly **hexagonal** (six-sided) in shape and fit neatly together. People of all ages enjoy jumping from rock to rock in this giant's playground!

The Giant's Causeway

Many legends try to explain how and why the Giant's Causeway came about. One legend is that Fionn MacCumhaill (McCool) started to build a causeway (bridge) across to Scotland. He wanted to fight a great Scottish giant. He then discovered that the Scottish giant was much bigger and stronger than him so he stopped building the causeway straight away!

Antrim

In fact, the stones in the Giant's Causeway were formed about 60 million years ago. At that time, there were active volcanoes in Antrim. The volcanoes erupted and lava poured out. When the lava hit the seawater, it cooled down quickly. Differences in how fast it cooled resulted in the famous columns. This happened on three separate occasions over the years.

As a result, the columns are different heights. They are known as the Lower, Middle and Upper Basalts. It is the middle basalt rocks which form the columns of the Giant's Causeway.

The Burren

The **Burren** is an area in County Clare in the west of Ireland. It is often described as having a **lunar** landscape. This is because it looks like the surface of the moon. It is an area of limestone rock with mountains and valleys.

Volcano erupting beside the sea

It is mostly bare rock and is full of holes. In spite of this, about 600 species of plants manage to grow there. Many of these species are not found anywhere else in Ireland.

The rock in the Burren is **limestone**. Water from the rain can **seep** through it, forming holes. Some holes in the Burren are very deep and have formed huge caves underground. **Potholers** like

The Burren

to explore these caves. Potholers have discovered incredible rock formations, like **stalagmites** and **stalactites**. They are formed by dripping water which contains lime. Stalactites appear to come out of the ceiling of a cave like an icicle. Stalagmites form upwards from the floor of a cave. The most famous caves in the Burren are the **Aillwee Caves**, which are open to visitors. They go deep into the ground. Bears used to live in these caves many years ago.

Clare

Potholer looking at rock formations

Stalactites

Stalagmites

The Skellig Islands

The two **Skellig Islands** lie off the coast of County Kerry in the Atlantic Ocean. They are pyramid-shaped and are mostly covered with bare rock. **Small Skellig** is the smaller of the two islands. It is home to many thousands of birds such as gannets and puffins.

Kerry

Skellig Michael (**Sceilig Mhichíl** in Irish) is the larger island. Centuries ago, it was home to monks, who wanted to leave the outside world behind and spend their lives in prayer. It was peaceful but life was very hard in this cold and isolated place.

The monks carved hundreds of steps into the cliff on Skellig Michael. These steps are the only way to get to the top of the island. The monks lived in tiny **beehive-shaped** huts made of stone.

Skellig Michael

Beehive-shaped hut on Skellig Michael

They fed themselves by keeping bees for honey and by catching fresh fish from the sea. They probably scrambled up and down the cliffs to get eggs from the nests of seabirds. It was very dangerous. In winter, wild storms blew in from the Atlantic Ocean. Even nowadays, Skellig Michael is a difficult place to visit. However, going there is a great adventure and is well worth the effort.

Activities

A **Talk about**

1 What do you think Ireland was like 60 million years ago?
2 Why do you think potholing is such a dangerous but exciting sport?
3 What do you think life was like for the monks on Skellig Michael?

B **What have you learned?**

1 In what county is the Giant's Causeway?
2 What shape are most of the rocks in the Giant's Causeway?
3 How were the rocks in the Giant's Causeway formed?
4 In what county is the Burren?
5 From what type of rock is the Burren made?
6 How do you think that 600 species of plants can grow there?
7 How are stalactites formed?
8 Name the most famous caves in Ireland.
9 Name the larger of the Skellig Islands.
10 Why do you think the monks built beehive-shaped huts?

C **Complete the sentences**

Fill in the blanks to complete the following sentences.

1 The _____ is in County Antrim.
2 The _____ is in County Clare.
3 The _____ are off the coast of County Kerry.
4 The _____ _____ is an ocean off the west coast of Ireland.

D **True or false**

1 The Giant's Causeway was built by a giant. _____
2 Bears once lived in the Aillwee Caves. _____
3 Monks used to live in caravans on Skellig Michael. _____
4 The Skellig Islands are in the Irish Sea. _____
5 The Giant's Causeway is made of limestone. _____

E (Write the questions)

Write the questions to match the following answers.

1 Q. _____?
  A. He wanted to fight the great Scottish Giant.

2 Q. _____?
  A. The Lower, Middle and Upper Basalts form the Giant's Causeway.

3 Q. _____?
  A. The most famous caves in the Burren are the Aillwee Caves.

4 Q. _____?
  A. The monks on Skellig Michael lived in beehive-shaped huts.

F (Mixed-up sentences)

Sort out the following mixed-up sentences.

1 The is an Burren in Clare. County area
2 Stalagmites form from the cave. upwards floor of the
3 got eggs nests The monks from seabirds. the of

G (Draw a picture)

Draw each of the following in your copy.

1 A rock from the Giant's Causeway.
2 A stalagmite and a stalactite.
3 Skellig Michael.

H (Finish the story)

Roger was walking across the Burren with his dog, Spot. Suddenly, Spot saw a rabbit and chased after it. The rabbit ran down a hole to escape, but Spot followed. Roger crawled into the hole to get Spot back, only to find himself inside a huge cave …

Notes